Berlitz®

USA

Road Trip 1980

NYC - CALI
TO MEXICO
TO ATLANTA
TO NYC

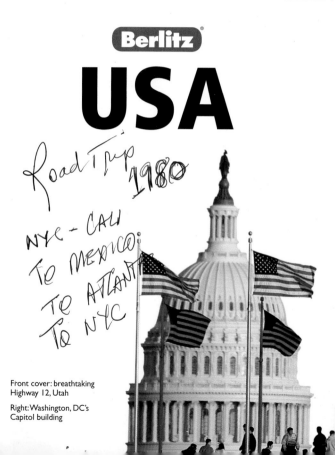

Front cover: breathtaking
Highway 12, Utah

Right: Washington, DC's
Capitol building

TOP 10 ATTRACTIONS

Colonial Virginia • Where American history was made *(page 100)*

Washington, DC • Packed with the historic monuments of US history, as well as some fine museums *(page 84)*

New York City • It still exerts its unique magnetism *(page 41)*

The Grand Canyon • Simply one of the greatest spectacles of nature on earth *(page 159)*

Las Vegas • Built on gambling, this city now offers much more with its astonishing theme hotels and dazzling shows *(page 194)*

San Francisco One of America's favorite cities, a vibrant melting pot with a stunning natural setting and the glorious Golden Gate Bridge *(page 166)*

New Orleans Despite awful flooding in 2005, it has retained its southern spirit *(page 121)*

Yosemite National Park It offers some of California's most impressive scenery, including the awesome face of 'El Capitan' *(page 190)*

Los Angeles Home to Tinseltown and as much a state of mind as a city *(page 180)*

Miami Beach Destination of sunseekers and home to fine Art Deco architecture *(page 105)*

CONTENTS

51

90

189

168

150

158

INTRODUCTION

The United States of America is still the 'New World' for anyone who hasn't visited here before. From the beckoning beacon of the Statue of Liberty in New York, all the way across the nation to the shiny palaces of technology in Seattle and California, America boldly leads the world into the 21st century.

Although a trip to the USA can take in some of the world's greatest waterfalls, ski resorts, coasts, deserts, and natural wonders, one striking facet of the inhabited parts of the States is the galloping pace of newness. Still a familiar greeting all over the United States is 'Hey, what's new?' New styles and forms of recreation are limitless in the playgrounds of Miami, Los Angeles, and Las Vegas. Experiments in social organization are in evidence from New York to Washington, DC, to San Francisco. Nobody knows better than Americans that all work and no play makes for a dull population, and so the United States is also the natural home of jeans, T-shirts, fast food, surfboards, and rollerblades.

Change and Progress

Change and progress are more than embraced here; they are craved and pursued. In almost every city, residential areas with architectural styles up to 100 years old surround the tall, gleaming pinnacles of downtown high-rise commercial districts. The diners and main streets of small-town USA seem to remain in a romantic time warp somewhere around the rock-and-roll era of the 1950s, until suddenly you notice that everybody is communicating on cellphones, and arranging their diaries on PDAs. Cars – big and outrageous or sleek and petite – are a wonder to behold. Not only that, but gas is inexpensive.

Yet some of the world's oldest, and greatest, natural phenomena are on display in forms as diverse as the vast Grand Canyon,

Monument Valley

white-hot Death Valley, shimmering Niagara Falls, the glorious Great Lakes, national parks of every conceivable description, and that 'Old Man River' itself, the mighty Mississippi that traverses most of the country from north to south.

Geography

With an area of approximately 3,717,700 sq. miles (9,629,000 sq. km), including Alaska and Hawaii, the US is the fourth-largest country in the world, or nearly 40 times the size of the UK. Mainland USA (excluding Alaska and Hawaii), called the 48 contiguous states, stretches for about 3,000 miles (4,800km) from the Atlantic to the Pacific oceans and for some 1,200 miles (1,900km) from the Canadian border to the Gulf of Mexico.

The largest state in the union is Alaska, nearly 152,000 sq. miles (1.4m sq. km). Hawaii, the 50th state, is located in the Pacific Ocean, some 2,500 miles (4,000km) to the southwest. The highest point is the summit of Mt McKinley (Alaska), 20,320ft

Come to Vegas for a slice of New York-New York

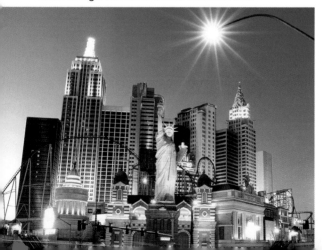

(6,194m). The lowest point is 282ft (86m) below sea level in Death Valley (California), the second-lowest point on dry land anywhere in the world.

Government and Population

The US is a federal republic consisting of 50 states and one federal district (Washington's District of Columbia – the 'DC' of the name). There is a two-party political system (the Democrats and the Republicans). The government is based on the Constitution of 1787.

A Florida fishing pier

The president is elected for a period of four years, and can be re-elected once. Congress is composed of the Senate (with two senators per state) and the House of Representatives (435 members, proportionately drawn from each state according to its population).

Each state has its own semiautonomous government and local laws, headed by a popularly elected governor. The population of 304 million, according to the 2007 *CIA Factbook*, is made up of 80 percent whites, 12.9 percent African-Americans, 4.4 percent Asians, 1 percent Native Americans, and a small percentage of other races. Just over 15 percent of the total population is Hispanic. Religious affiliation is thought to be 51.3 percent Protestant, 23.9 percent Roman Catholic, 16.1 percent none or unaffiliated, 1.7 percent Jewish, 1.7 percent Mormon, and 2.5 percent other.

Culture

Other countries display their glorious past in museums, cathedrals, temples, and palaces. America shows off and shares its exuberant present – but in the street and on the beach. Other countries talk

**Inside New York's
Guggenheim Museum**

of their culture; America welcomes visitors to its way of life. The days when Europeans might hazard a patronizing observation on America's cultural life should be well and truly over by now. In fields like classical music, opera, and the visual arts, the United States can give a good account of itself in any company.

The Arts

America is home to seven world-famous symphony orchestras and opera companies, in Chicago, New York, Los Angeles, Philadelphia, Cleveland, Washington, DC, and Boston. The endlessly innovative paintings and sculptures of Manhattan and California are regularly featured among the world's leading art movements.

The great museums of New York, Washington, and Chicago stand among the world's finest. Nationwide, American architecture is forever seeking and finding novel solutions, contributing to the inspirational traditions from Frank Lloyd Wright to Frank Gehry to Daniel Libeskind, major architect of the new design for New York's World Trade Center site.

The architecture of America is often superb, occasionally startling, but never timid, addressing the problems of urban working and living space in an overcrowded age.

The Great Outdoors

Americans were clearly the spoiled children of creation when it came to distributing the bounty of the earth, and have in their easy reach a fantastic diversity of landscapes to which they can escape. The country's environmental reawakening started just in time to preserve much of the natural beauty of the continent's wide open spaces.

For sailors and anyone who likes to fish, there are the wild Atlantic coasts of Maine and Florida as well as their Pacific counterparts in northern California, Oregon, and Washington state. There are also the calmer waters of Long Island Sound and Chesapeake Bay, or the lazy beaches of the Gulf Coast and southern California. In between are the Great Lakes of the Midwest, which might easily qualify as seas anywhere else in the world.

National Parks

Throughout the country are great national parks and nature reserves, luring visitors to hike around the swamps of Florida's Everglades and climb in the White Mountains of New Hampshire, the Great Smokies of North Carolina and Tennessee, or the Rockies of Colorado. The vast parks of the West, with the geysers, waterfalls, and evergreen forest of Wyoming's Yellowstone; the

El Capitan in California's Yosemite National Park

rainbow canyons of Utah's Zion; the massive redwoods of northern California, the stupendous rock faces of Yosemite; and, of course, Arizona's Grand Canyon, all offer sanctuaries in which to enjoy the natural beauty that contains the soul of this industrial giant. Even the deserts – the Petrified Forest southeast of the Grand Canyon, or Death Valley in California's Mojave – grant an enriching respite from civilization.

City Life

But civilization American-style is just too much fun to stay away from for too long. Each of the major cities offers its own adventure. The street life of New York is a carnival – endless movement, color, noise, taste, and aroma – sometimes hair-raising, always stimulating. Boston, Washington, and Philadelphia are metropolitan pillars of American history, proud and dignified towns that don't take themselves too seriously. New Orleans offers a deliciously exotic jambalaya of old elegance and decadence, part Gallic, part Deep South, but always vibrant and musical. Santa Fe is its Spanish counterpart, but quieter, more the culture of fine arts than the romance of jazz. There's nothing quiet or delicate about big, boisterous Chicago, however. The town never fails to surprise visitors with the beauty of its lakefront architecture, or the breadth and exuberance of its musical heritage.

Washington, DC's Capitol building

Dallas and Houston are the bumptious concrete realizations of the Texan dream, ranchers gone oil-rich urban. These same ranchers fly to chic, sun-drenched Miami to realize yet more dreams (and to spend some of those riches in South Beach's chic stores and restaurants). Star-mad Los

Manhattan from the Empire State Building

Angeles and gorgeous, nonconformist San Francisco are the last extravagant points on the map of America's big push to the western coast. Big and small, America's cities are both playgrounds and workshops displaying the best, and some of the worse, aspects of a century of tireless urban development.

Fantasy Playgrounds

If you're exhausted from taking in the wonders of the real world, you can revel in the fantasy realms of Universal Studios and Disneyland, or the sinful glamor of Las Vegas and other resorts that have burst glittering across the country. The thrills and excitement are carefully designed not to create too much stress – all good clean family fun (apart from Las Vegas, of course; Sin City obeys few rules). Children have an important place in local life, and Americans have long understood that all of us, some of the time – perhaps more often than we are willing to admit – are children.

Americans love to play. Their own versions of old European sports – baseball (which an American encyclopedia admits is

Looking to the future

'doubtless derived' from English cricket and rounders) and what they call football, which looks to foreign eyes like a contest that might easily have been invented for Roman gladiators – are exuberant spectacles. In addition to the spectator sports are the endless fads that spring up around the beaches of Florida, California, and Hawaii – surfing, rollerblading, parascending, and sand yachting – all come and go with the swift arc of a frisbee.

Diversity

In a country as vast and varied as the United States, it is hazardous to try to pin down the catch-all moniker of 'Americans.' White Anglo-Saxon Protestants? Irish Catholics? Hispanics, Poles, Italians, Germans, Greeks, Arabs, Scandinavians, Russians, Jews, Czechs, Africans, Chinese, Japanese, Vietnamese, or Sioux, Navajo, Cherokee, and Cheyenne? Or, for that matter, New Yorkers and New Englanders, Southerners and Texans, Midwesterners and hillbillies, and again, to confound all generalizations – Californians? It's worth making out this long and far from exhaustive list just to be able to contemplate the incredible diversity of these people collectively called Americans.

And then you realize that this is the answer. This is the valid definition of 'Americans;' they are this culture of boundless variety. Somehow people from every far-flung corner of the earth have ended up living together – not always peacefully by any means – but despite revolution and civil war and riots, with such astounding success.

Perhaps the greatest adventure of your American journey will be to encounter as many as you can of the different people making up these United States: cool New Englanders, pushy New Yorkers, bluff and hearty Texans, earnest Midwestern farmers – and their exact opposites, for no generalization stands up to more than five minutes' scrutiny in this super-country.

Discovery

Wherever you discover Americans, you'll be sure to see that they have not coalesced into a dull, homogeneous nation of look-alikes, talk-alikes, and laugh-alikes. Martin Luther King, Jr, was right to contest the image of America as a melting pot. He said it was in fact a good bowl of vegetable soup in which you could taste the carrots, potatoes, leeks, and peas, all separately, and all together.

The one thing you can say for sure is that every time you visit, you'll find that the recipe has been varied, spiced, and flavored again and again.

Freedom on the road

A BRIEF HISTORY

For at least 25,000, maybe as many as 40,000, years, at a time when mammoth and bison left Siberia for new pastures across a now submerged land bridge over the Bering Strait, North America has been inhabited by man. Mongolian hunters, probable ancestors of later Indian tribes, followed the bison into what is now Alaska.

Over the centuries, some made their way down the Pacific Coast and east across the continent. Between 500BC and AD500, the Hopi and Zuni settled in farming communities in adobe-walled *pueblos* of New Mexico and Arizona. By 1500, the only truly no-madic tribes were the Plains Indians who roamed between the Rockies and the Mississippi River forests. Tribes along the East Coast were skilled farmers, but they had no wheel, no metal tools, and no horses. Their only beasts of burden were dogs.

The Europeans Arrive

The first non-tribesmen were Norsemen from Greenland, who crossed to Newfoundland between 1001 and 1015. Then they dis-appeared again without trace.

Not so the Spanish. It was 10pm on October 11, 1492, when the Genoese captain acting for the Spanish monarchy, Christopher Columbus, stood with his watchman looking at a pale light on the western horizon. It turned out to be on an island in the Bahamas, just 380 miles (612km) from what centuries later became Miami Beach. Although Columbus was to die almost penniless, he is the man credited with discovering America.

Five years later, another Genoese-born sailor, John Cabot, set foot in Newfoundland, stopping just long enough to stake the fateful Eng-lish claim to North America for his king, Henry VII. But it was the name of a third Italian explorer, Amerigo Vespucci, that was used by a mapmaker and stuck to both northern and southern continents.

Signing the Declaration of Independence

The first European contact with the future United States mainland came in 1513, when Spanish explorer Juan Ponce de León was searching for the Fountain of Youth and stumbled upon the coast of Florida. In 1565, the Spaniards built a fort nearby at what is now St Augustine, the first permanent settlement.

The English began to explore seriously in 1607. After cursory examination of what was to become California and some unsuccessful efforts on the East Coast, they established their first settlement at Jamestown, Virginia. Then on November 11, 1620, over 100 people fleeing from religious persecution sighted Cape Cod, Massachusetts, while aboard the *Mayflower*. The seeds of American democracy were contained in a covenant drawn up by these 'pilgrims' – the *Mayflower Compact*, which provided that laws accepted by the majority would be binding on all. They founded a community at Plymouth Bay, learning from friendly tribes how to fish and plant maize. Half the pilgrims died that first hard winter. After the harvest, the survivors and 90 Wampanoag Indians held a feast of wild turkey and waterfowl – one of the first Thanksgivings.

Making contact with the natives

In 1626, the Manhattan Indians sold their island to the Dutch West India Company for the legendary sum of $24, and New Amsterdam sprang up as a classic seaman's town of taverns and seedy hangouts for smugglers and illicit traders. Apart from a few farms, or *bouweries*, the Dutch didn't invest much in their American property, concentrating their energies on the

East Indies. Smart New Englanders moved down to Westchester and Long Island, and the English began putting pressure on the Dutch to move out. In 1664, with the British fleet in the harbor, Dutch governor Peter Stuyvesant allowed New Amsterdam to become New York without a shot being fired. Some Dutch families remained, however, including the Roosevelts, who later went on to produce US two presidents.

Free Penn

In 1681, William Penn set up a colony in Philadelphia. This energetic Quaker from London established the proprietary province of Pennsylvania as a haven of free enterprise and religious tolerance. Swedes, Finns, and Dutch already settled there were now joined by farmers from England, France, and Germany.

Toward Revolution

As the British empire expanded in the middle of the 18th century, the monarchy demanded that the American colonies contribute more to its upkeep and defense. While accepting royal authority in foreign affairs, the colonists assumed they would enjoy the same freedoms and privileges as other Englishmen. But between 1764 and 1767 a series of special taxes (on newspapers and legal documents) and import duties (on sugar, silk, linen, Madeira wine, paint, lead, paper, and tea) made them realize they weren't just Englishmen abroad. A South Carolina leader, Christopher Gadsden, drew the inevitable conclusion: 'There ought to be no New England men, no New Yorkers known on the continent, but all of us Americans.'

Groups known as the 'Sons of Liberty' formed in New York and Boston, attacked the royal tax collectors' houses, and burned their furniture. In Boston the propagandist and agitator Samuel Adams led dances around the Liberty Tree, an elm from which unpopular officials were hanged in effigy. As unrest mounted, the British sent two regiments to Boston. In March 1770, a mob snowballed guards in front of the Boston Customs House. The attack grew fierce and the British fired, killing four Bostonians.

Boston Tea Party

With most of the offending duties repealed, three years of peace and prosperity followed. But the duty on tea remained. While Philadelphia and New York staged boycotts, Sam Adams's Sons of Liberty (disguised as Mohawk Indians) boarded three British ships in Boston Harbor and dumped the cargo in the sea. The Boston Tea Party of 1773 moved George III to say: 'The colonies must either submit or triumph.' The Americans agreed.

The American colonies called their First Continental Congress in Philadelphia in September 1774 to coordinate opposition. Again, Massachusetts took the lead, declaring itself a 'free state' and prepared to resist any British offensive with weapons and ammunition stored at Concord. The British moved 12,000 troops to Boston and, in April 1775, a contingent marched out to deal with the rebels. Paul Revere, as legend has it, rode 'through every Middlesex village and farm' to warn of the British advance on Concord. The first resistance was at Lexington, but it was on the bridge

The Boston Tea Party

at Concord that 'embattled farmers' faced the British and 'fired the shot heard 'round the world.'

Despite the Second Continental Congress's push for independence – led by Massachusetts's John Hancock, Virginia's Thomas Jefferson, and Pennsylvania's Benjamin Franklin – many were still reluctant to sever ties with Britain. On July 4, 1776, though, the Declaration of Independence was signed, proclaiming 'life, liberty and the pursuit of happiness.' The war dragged on for seven years, patriot farmers engaging the British in skirmishes, in a morale-sapping battle of strategic attrition. After the Battle of Long Island in August 1776, the British took control of New York for the rest of the war. Philadelphia fell in September 1777, leaving George Washington and his depleted forces to shiver out the winter in nearby Valley Forge.

The British assumed control of the Atlantic Coast, gaining victories at Savannah and Charleston. Then American troops forged north to Virginia, taking command of British outposts along the way. There, French support paid off in a combined action with Washington in which 15,000 men won the decisive Battle of Yorktown. On October 17, 1781, Lord Cornwallis's British soldiers surrendered. After two years of negotiations led by Benjamin Franklin, the Peace of Paris ended the Revolutionary War on September 3, 1783.

The New Republic Expands Westward

New York was the first capital of the new United States of America, and it was on a balcony overlooking Wall Street on April 30, 1789, that George Washington was inaugurated as president. Endowed with great character, he made up for his lack of political talent by surrounding himself with men who possessed it in abundance, among them Thomas Jefferson as Secretary of State and Alexander Hamilton at the Treasury. His vice-president was John Adams – cousin of Sam, the Boston Tea Party troublemaker. As champion of a new democracy, Jefferson was disturbed by an obstacle on his own doorstep. The United States' first census (1790) showed a population of nearly 4 million, of whom 700,000 were black slaves. Himself a slave-owner on his Virginia farm, Jefferson expressed hopes for 'a total emancipation,' fearing trouble for the union of the states if this did not occur.

Jefferson was elected president in 1800, and early the next year was the first to be inaugurated in the new capital, the town of Washington on the Potomac River along the eastern seaboard. Apart from the White House and the Capitol, this was little more than a collection of ramshackle boarding houses, where many senators and congressmen had to bed down on the floor.

One of the major triumphs of the Jefferson presidency was the Louisiana Purchase of 1803. The French territory stretched from the Mississippi River to the Rocky Mountains, 828,000 sq. miles (2,144,520 sq. km) that more than doubled the size of the country. Preoccupied with an insurrection in Haiti and his war with the British, Napoleon sold the land for $15 million. The next year, Captain Meriwether Lewis and Lieutenant William Clark set out from St Louis to explore the uncharted West all the way to the Pacific Ocean.

The expedition was intended not only to lay American claim to the Oregon territory but also to size up the 'Indian situation' in the Northwest. Many suspected that the British were encouraging the tribes to resist American western expansion. This and disputes over free trade rights during Britain's naval blockade of Napoleon led, under President James Madison, to another war with the British, from 1812 to 1814. The US invaded Canada, killing the great tribe leader Tecumseh and burning parliamentary houses in York (later Toronto). The British retaliated at Fort Niagara and Buffalo. Washington was attacked and the White House was set on fire.

Pushing West

Under President Andrew Jackson, the American frontier was pushed to the West. Trappers and fur-hunters led the new pioneers from the Missouri River to the Rockies during the 1830s. In canvas-covered wagons known as 'prairie schooners,' thousands of backwoodsmen set out for Oregon in the 1840s. America's drive to the Pacific Ocean was proclaimed to be the nation's 'manifest destiny.' Other Americans moved beyond the United States' frontiers to Mexican-owned

Covered wagons on the Oregon Trail

Texas. By 1836 they were 20,000 strong, outnumbering the Mexicans there by four to one. They liked Mexican horsemanship, saddles, and trappings, but rebelled against the authoritarian government. After fierce fighting in retaliation for the Mexican massacre of Americans at the Alamo, Texas was made an independent 'Lone Star Republic.' In 1845 it was annexed to the US.

The Civil War

Throughout the era of western expansion, the slavery issue festered. Slaves made up 40 percent of the southern states' population. As long as cotton was 'king,' representing two-thirds of US exports, the South felt it could justify working slaves on the plantations. When rebellions broke out in South Carolina and Virginia, repression was ruthless, and strict curfews were put in place. Owners organized night patrols, and teaching slaves to read or write was strictly forbidden.

In the North, the Abolitionist movement grew to 200,000 by 1840. Since slave owners could legally reclaim fugitives in the northern states, an 'Underground Railroad' was organized to help slaves escape north into Canada. By the 1850s, any lingering moral considerations the South may have had were blurred by the purely political issue of states' rights. The slave-owning states insisted on the right to decide their own affairs without the interference of the federal government.

A new Republican Party was founded in 1854 on an anti-slavery platform and, by the 1860 presidential elections, was firmly identified with the North. The Democrats split on the issue of whether the new western territories should be obliged to permit slavery, and southern states fielded their own candidate in addition to the Democrats' official nominee. The Republicans chose Abraham Lincoln, a man of homespun personality who could get enough support in the new Midwestern states to guarantee victory over the divided Democrats.

South Carolina led Mississippi, Alabama, Florida, Georgia, Louisiana, and Texas into secession from the Union. The reason was that the North had elected 'a man whose opinions and purposes are hostile to slavery.' In fact, Lincoln's aims were not so simple. As he wrote to a New York editor: 'My paramount object

Indian Country

The battle for the land and its riches had been waged against Native American tribes ever since Europeans first set foot on American soil. It reached its climax after the Civil War, when the government set out finally to 'conquer' the West and force the tribes onto reservations. Despite victories like the Battle of the Little Bighorn, the invasion by the white man was unstoppable, a fact well understood by Chief Joseph of the Nez Perce as he pondered the plight of his people:

'I have carried a heavy load on my back ever since I was a boy. I realized then that we could not hold our own with the white men. We were like deer. They were like grizzly bears. We had small country. Their country was large. We were contented to let things remain as the Great Spirit Chief made them. They were not, and would change the rivers and mountains if they did not suit them.'

in this struggle is to save the Union and not either to save or destroy slavery.' But he had said earlier: 'I believe this government cannot endure permanently half *slave* and half *free*.'

Manning the guns during the Civil War

In February 1861, the Confederate States of America elected as their president Jefferson Davis, an aristocratic ex-soldier. Arkansas, Tennessee, Virginia, and North Carolina joined the Confederacy, but Kentucky, Missouri, Maryland, and Delaware did not. Virginia's great military leader, General Robert E. Lee, was more ambivalent than the politicians. 'I can contemplate no greater calamity for the country,' he wrote in January 1861, 'than a dissolution of the Union. Still, a Union that can only be maintained by swords and bayonets and in which strife and civil war are to take the place of brotherly love or kindness, has no charm for me.' This troubled hero emancipated his slaves but joined the southern cause.

On April 12, 1861, South Carolina troops opened fire on the US military base of Fort Sumter, and the Civil War began. The four-year war was a horror. Grand moments of heroism in the battles of Antietam (Maryland), Gettysburg (Pennsylvania), Fredericksburg (Virginia), Shiloh (Tennessee), and Vicksburg (Mississippi) were mere punctuation marks, however glorious, in the cold, wet, disease-ridden guerrilla-style conflict. More than twice as many died from dysentery, typhoid, malaria, and consumption as were killed by bullets and bayonets.

The South had proud military traditions, superior officers and training, but the North had overwhelming supremacy in heavy industry, railways, and arms. It triumphed despite often incompetent military leadership. While Lee brought classical elegance and Thomas 'Stonewall' Jackson a fatalistic realism to southern generalship, the North's Ulysses Grant and William Sherman demonstrated relentless willpower and brute force. After Grant occupied the Confederate capital of Richmond, Virginia, Lee submitted the South's surrender at Appomattox on April 9, 1865. Just five days later, Lincoln was assassinated at Ford's Theater in Washington by the actor and Confederate sympathizer John Wilkes Booth.

Reconstruction

Ravaged by the war, its major cities reduced to rubble, Georgia in ruin from Atlanta to Savannah, the Southern economy was shattered, its banks insolvent. The cotton crop of 1860 was not matched again till 1879. As the planter-aristocracy moved out, either to the North and West or abroad to England, Mexico, or Brazil, poor white farmers took over. The North had prospered, the war having produced a new class of millionaire – Rockefeller in oil, Remington in guns (later typewriters). Over 800,000 immigrants streamed into the North during the war and over 3 million more followed in the next 10 years.

African-Americans, 4 million freed by the Union's victory, faced more hardships. After the first euphoria they woke to the embittered South's new 'black codes' under which they could not vote, testify against whites, bear arms, or frequent public places reserved for whites. The Washington government could not make good on the '40 acres and a mule' which had been promised each freed slave. The most positive achievement of the Freedmen's Bureau was to set up new hospitals and schools. But many African-Americans also faced greater violence than they had ever known as slaves, and the Ku Klux Klan, founded in Tennessee in 1866, spread terror throughout the South.

The federal government's Reconstruction Acts replaced recalcitrant southern-state governments with Northerners and African-Americans, backed by federal troops, to guarantee 'equal protection of the laws.' However, under Rutherford Hayes, the Enforcement Acts were nullified, and for three generations southern African-Americans were in limbo.

The World Stage

By 1914, America had established itself as the world's leading industrial power. The railroad, steel, coal, oil, and vast agricultural resources brought unprecedented wealth.

From 1860 to 1920, the population more than tripled, from 31 million to 106 million. This was a period of massive immigration: 4 million British, 4 million Irish, 6 million Germans, over 2 million Scandinavians, plus Italians, Poles, Czechs, Austrians, Hungarians, Serbs, and Russian Jews. Northern Europeans went West, to the farmlands; Southern and Eastern Europeans and the Irish mainly stuck to the big Eastern and Midwestern cities. Jews went into the garment industry, Finns into the mines, Portuguese into textiles. The Chinese worked in the mines and on the railways – and suffered from anti-Oriental laws when white Americans became scared for their jobs.

Fresh arrivals in New York in the late 19th century

The trade union movement – or organized labor, as it is known in the US – demanded its share of the profits. This proved hard, and the strikes, lockouts, and pitched battles between workers and company militia were violent.

America bought Alaska from Russia in 1867 and absorbed Hawaii by negotiating trading and military privileges with the strategically vital Pacific islands. In the Caribbean, the US proved itself adept at gunboat diplomacy. In the 1898 war against the Spanish, America ended up in charge of Puerto

Rico and Guam (in the Pacific), military occupation of the Philippines, and the role of godfather to Cuba's independence.

As older nations fought on the battlefields of Europe, America prepared for the world stage. Woodrow Wilson, son of a southern Presbyterian minister, brought a decidedly moral and didactic flavor to the presidency. After helping the Allies to victory over Germany, Wilson presented at the Versailles peace negotiations an elaborate plan for a League of Nations.

Boomtime and the Great Depression

After the Russian Revolution, America succumbed to a Communist scare. The New York state legislature expelled five Socialist members because of their politics, and in 1927, two Italian-born anarchists charged with murdering a shoe-factory paymaster in Massachusetts were executed. Many held that the jury was swayed more by its fear of anarchic politics than by its conviction of criminal responsibility. But the 1920s were also when the good times rolled: jazz, radio, silent movies, and cars – 26 million of them by the end of the decade. Materialism was respectable. As President Calvin Coolidge put it: 'The business of America is business' – and it was enjoying a boom.

The growth of the big cities with their exotic immigrant populations brought a threat to the old American rural and small-town principles. Prohibition of alcohol in 1920 was justified with moral argument, but far from upholding morality, Prohibition promoted gangland crime. In 1928, Herbert Hoover, a humanitarian in World War I and the candidate of American business, arrived in the White House with high hopes: 'Poverty will be banished from this nation.'

But the next year came the Great Crash of the New York Stock Exchange and America slumped into the Depression. Between 1929 and 1932, 5,000 banks closed down. One-third of the population were either unemployed by 1933, or members of families whose breadwinner was out of work. People went hungry while fruit, vegetables, and grain were in abundance. Houses were unheated while coal piled up. America was stunned by the failure of its classic virtues: business leadership, organization, and efficiency.

The Mob found legitimacy in early Las Vegas

In 1933, Franklin D. Roosevelt embarked on a whirlwind 'Hundred Days' of economic and social measures to conquer the catastrophe. With a canny sense of public relations, the president confided in the people with radio 'fireside chats,' and cheered them up by legalizing wine and beer as Prohibition was dismantled.

FDR's 'New Deal' did beat back the disaster of the Depression, but economic recession did not end till World War II.

World War II and Beyond

After Woodrow Wilson's internationalist approach, America preferred the comforts of isolation. Even FDR said in 1936: 'We shun political commitments which might entangle us in foreign wars.' But this neutralist policy was revoked after Hitler's 1940 *Blitzkrieg* against Belgium, France, and the Netherlands. Congress supplied arms and aid to its allies – but still resisted conscription. The Japanese raid on Pearl Harbor, on December 7, 1941, ended all hesitation.

Roosevelt was re-elected to an unprecedented fourth term in 1944, but after a long struggle with infantile paralysis, he died in

The *Arizona* is sunk at Pearl Harbor

April 1945, before the final victory. Harry Truman made the decision to use an atom bomb to end the war with Japan.

After World War II, America emerged as the only major power undamaged by the conflict. In fact, the US economy had grown: American corporations like Boeing and General Electric, as well as Coca-Cola and the movie business of Hollywood, all had a 'good war' and came out prosperous. Times at home were good for most, although the inequalities and ethnic tensions inbuilt in the Land of the Free were set to bring domestic conflict during these 'peace years.'

Civil Rights

The 1950s were a brash, confident decade of prosperity and possibility. Cars were big, clothes were sharp, and disc jockey Alan Freed coined the term 'rock and roll' to make black rhythm and blues accessible to white audiences. Elvis Aaron Presley stepped into Sam Phillips's Sun Studios in Memphis with a disc he'd cut in a recording booth, and from then on, teenaged girls reeled each time he swiveled his hips.

Halfway through the decade, in 1955, President Eisenhower sent the first 'military advisors' to Vietnam. The same year Dr Martin Luther King, Jr led the first black bus boycott, and the next year, the Supreme Court outlawed segregation on buses. The march for black equal rights was on.

On September 2, 1957, nine black students were due to start their new school year in Little Rock, Arkansas. As theirs was a newly desegregated school, passions boiled around the issue, and the National Guard were called out to protect the school. Initially they prevented the students from entering. It took 23 days, 10,000 National Guardsmen, 1,000 paratroops, a court injunction, and the intervention of Eisenhower himself before the students were able to start lessons. The issues of desgregation and equality of citizenship rumbled on until the Civil Rights Act of 1964, with some of the scars still visible today.

> **Alaska and Hawaii**
>
> At the end of the 1950s, the United States was still growing in size, as well as in stature. Alaska and Hawaii became the 49th and 50th states in 1959.

The Kennedy Era

At the beginning of the 1960s, John F. Kennedy was elected president, narrowly beating Richard Nixon. After a tough time with the press in the campaign, Nixon conceded, saying, 'You won't have Nixon to push around any more.' Not his last public pronouncement that would turn out to be untrue. As a gesture of American can-do grit, President Kennedy committed the US to putting a man on the moon by the end of the decade.

Kennedy, with his brother Bobby as Attorney General, presided in dangerous times. Bobby tried to fight organized crime in the teeth of opposition from the Director of the FBI, J. Edgar Hoover. Hoover said that the real threat was from the 'enemy within,' the Red Peril (meaning Communists). Meanwhile, JFK had to deal with 'real reds' just across the sea from Miami, in Fidel Castro's Cuba. Perhaps acting on poor advice, Kennedy committed 1,600 CIA-trained insurgents to invade Cuba. They were easily defeated with massive losses, and the result was known as the Bay of Pigs fiasco.

Perhaps emboldened, Russia stationed missiles at bases in Cuba. They were detected by American reconnaissance flights, and on April 22, 1962, Kennedy demanded them withdrawn. He mounted a naval and air blockade, and the world held its breath for six days. In exchange for a face-saving promise not to invade Cuba, Russian Premier Khrushchev removed the missiles.

With the prosperity of the 1960s, America's mood was one where the problem of how to survive seemed to have been solved. Collective thoughts now turned towards how to live. In 1962, women's rights activist and journalist Betty Friedan published *The Feminine Mystique*. She founded the National Organization for Women in 1966, but it still took until 1974 for an equal pay act to be issued from the Supreme Court. The 1960s Civil Rights movement swept the nation, as did the anti-war movement, both espoused by the hippies and flower children of California.

Love and Death

In the mid-1960s, San Francisco became the center of a hippie revolution. By 1967, the Haight-Ashbury neighborhood was thronged with long-haired young men and women promoting free love and a philosophy that basically said 'let it be,' culminating in a globally recognized 'Summer of Love.' But the 1960s was also a decade of violent political unrest. John F. Kennedy was shot dead in Dallas, Texas, on November 22, 1963. Lee Harvey Oswald was held to have been the lone assassin, but he, too, was murdered by nightclub owner and sometime FBI informant Jack Ruby, long before any trial could be brought. Martin Luther King, Jr was killed in Memphis, Tennessee, on April 4, 1968, prompting riots in more than 100 US cities. Just a month later, Bobby Kennedy was gunned down after a campaign address in Los Angeles.

1968 was also the year in which Richard Milhous Nixon made his second – this time successful – bid for the White House. Nixon, like his predecessors, promised an early end to American partici-

MLK gives his 'I have a dream' speech, Washington, DC, 1963

pation in the Vietnam War. Like presidents before him, he found it a tough promise to deliver. Still, Nixon was able to deliver on one of Kennedy's dreams: on July 20, 1969, Neil Armstrong stepped out of the *Apollo 11* lunar module onto the surface of the moon.

Nixon's second term of presidency was hopelessly mired in the scandal and criminal proceedings from a burglary at the Watergate building in Washington, DC. It was the vice-president, Gerald Ford, who was able to declare the final withdrawal from Vietnam on May 7, 1975. When Nixon himself was forced to resign over the Watergate affair, Ford took over the Oval Office.

The 1970s to 1990s

Hopeful of consigning scandals and disgrace to the past, in 1976 America chose a little-known peanut farmer from Georgia as its president. Jimmy Carter's term saw a nuclear incident at Three Mile Island and the deepening of a world oil crisis that had begun in 1973. However, he established full diplomatic relations with China, and began a hopeful peace process for the Middle East. But Carter's presidency was marred by the taking in Tehran of around 70 American hostages. For 444 days the story was at the top of every US news broadcast. Carter tried diplomacy and an abortive rescue attempt.

By coincidence or careful plotting, depending on your point of view, the hostages were finally released on the day of Ronald Reagan's inauguration as the 40th president in 1981. In 1986, Reagan admitted having secretly sold arms to Iran in what became known as the Iran-Contra scandal.

The tenure of Reagan's vice-president and successor, George H.W. Bush, was marked by the Gulf War in 1991, and still more race riots in 1992. He was also able to turn the economy around, but most of the credit went to the 42nd president, Bill Clinton.

The 1980s and 1990s saw another migration west, as thousands of Americans left the chilly winds and the uncertain economics of the East Coast to test their future on the sunny shores of California. West Coast businesses began to nurture cooperation with what became known as the 'Pacific Rim,' America's West Coast, and those parts of Asia bordering the Pacific Ocean. Traditional Pacific Northwest industries – lumber, agriculture, and fishing – took second place to shipping and light manufacturing opportunities with Asia, kindling interest in Seattle, Washington, and Portland, Oregon. At the same time, a former orchard-filled area called the Santa Clara Valley, south of San Francisco, was to be reborn as Silicon Valley.

The Rise of the Internet

Toward the end of the 20th century, American ingenuity brought a revolution to the world of commerce and communications with a legacy from the Cold War missile program. The ARPA net was a system of telephone connections that would automatically reroute to avoid any kind of damage, ensuring connections in an attack. Computer scientists in the 1980s realized that this knowledge enabled them to link computers almost anywhere, using public phone lines.

This was the birth of the internet, e-mail and the world wide web. The opportunity for individuals to communicate instantly and inexpensively changed the way that businesses, news-gatherers, and eventually just plain folk were able to talk.

The American spirit of entrepreneurship saw a pot of gold at the end of the internet rainbow, and investors poured billions of dollars into thousands of dot-com dreams. Seattle, Portland, San Francisco, and the Silicon Valley boomed. Expectations rose, results were slow, and a crash was inevitable. Just as slender ideas had been over-valued, even so-solid companies were destroyed.

Into the 21st Century

In November 2000, Clinton's vice-president, Al Gore, stood against George Bush's son, George W. Bush. The ballot

The horror of 9/11

was so close that it couldn't be decided by counting votes alone. A ruling of the Supreme Court finally gave the presidency to Bush.

A few months later, tragedy struck. On September 11, 2001, terrorists hijacked four aircraft full of passengers. One plane was flown into the Pentagon in Washington, and two more into the twin towers of the World Trade Center in New York. The fourth plane came down on open ground in Pennsylvania. Close to 3,000 innocent people were killed, and Bush declared a 'War on Terrorism.' Fear and panic struck America, perhaps for the first time. The economy shuttered.

More shareholder disasters came when huge corporations like Enron and Worldcom were shown to have connived with auditors to mislead the market over their true value, and Bush promised a 'new era of integrity.' Sadness struck at the American consciousness again on February 1, 2003, when during re-entry, the space shuttle *Columbia* disintegrated over Texas with the loss of all seven of the crew. The following month, without the support of the UN, American and British forces attacked Iraq.

In 2005, Hurricane Katrina ripped through the southern Gulf Coast states, causing devastation and the deaths of thousands of people. Rescue attempts were inept, and Americans were horrified by how ill-prepared their country was during a large-scale emergency.

The Audacity of Hope

In late 2008, a youthful, Harvard-educated senator from Chicago, Barack Obama, became the first African-American to be elected to the US presidency. Black people around the globe took this as a sign that their time had come at last. Taking a cue from the title of his memoir, *The Audacity of Hope*, Obama promised to 're-claim the American dream,' which had become tarnished after eight years under the Bush administration.

Amid the widespread jubilation, though, was the recognition that Obama's task was monumental: a global financial crisis had plunged the US into a downward economic spiral, requiring a bailout on the part of the federal government to the tune of billions of dollars. It

President Barack Obama

was a pensive, more grown-up country that witnessed Obama's inauguration in 2009.

Times have been turbulent, but the US always seems to bounce back. New architecture, like the revamped Museum of Modern Art in New York and Frank Gehry's Disney Concert Hall in Los Angeles, dazzle the eye and provide a glimpse of an optimistic future full of possibility. Much like the country itself, as a matter of fact.

Historical Landmarks

1492 Explorer Christopher Columbus reaches America.

1620 Pilgrims aboard the *Mayflower* arrive at Cape Cod.

1773 In the Boston Tea Party, tea crates are pitched over the sides of three ships in Boston Harbor to protest against taxes.

1776 On July 4, the Continental Congress in Philadelphia adopts the Declaration of Independence, penned by Thomas Jefferson.

1789 George Washington takes the first presidential oath at New York's Federal Hall.

1804 Lewis and Clark set out on their 8,000-mile (13,000km) expedition across America to the Pacific Coast.

1848 Gold is discovered at Sutter's Fort, California, bringing over 200,000 prospectors within the next three years.

1861 Confederates open fire on Fort Sumter, in the first shots of the Civil War.

1865 The Civil War ends. Abraham Lincoln is assassinated.

1929 Wall Street crashes, and with it comes the beginning of the Depression.

1941 Japan attacks Pearl Harbor, and the United States enters World War II.

1945 The first atomic bomb is detonated in New Mexico; bombs are dropped on Hiroshima and Nagasaki.

1955 Dr Martin Luther King, Jr leads the Montgomery (Alabama) bus boycott.

1963 President John F. Kennedy is assassinated in Dallas, Texas.

1968 Dr Martin Luther King, Jr and Robert F. Kennedy are assassinated.

1969 *Apollo 11* takes two men to the surface of the moon.

1973–4 A world oil crisis plunges the US into economic crisis.

1989 An earthquake, 7.1 on the Richter scale, collapses a freeway and causes chaos in the San Francisco area.

1991 American-led forces liberate Kuwait in the first Gulf War.

2000 The presidential election is undecided by counting votes, so the Supreme Court gives the presidency to George W. Bush.

2001 Hijackers fly passenger airliners into New York's World Trade Center and the Pentagon. A 'War on Terrorism' is declared.

2005 Hurricane Katrina hits the Gulf Coast states, killing thousands.

2008 The government injects billions of dollars into the ailing economy.

2009 The US's first African-American president, Barack Obama, takes office.

WHERE TO GO

A trip to the United States is the gateway to a wealth of travel opportunity. Almost every imaginable kind of landscape, outdoor activity, and entertainment is available, many times over. From the natural wonders of the Grand Canyon, the Great Lakes and the mountains and coasts of the Pacific, to the megalopolises of New York, Las Vegas, and Miami, America has almost everything that the modern or the natural world can offer. You can enjoy whale-watching in Oregon, skiing in the Rockies, or café society in San Francisco. See unrivaled shows and gamble in Las Vegas, or watch world-class theater between shopping forays in Manhattan. America is the fourth-largest country on earth, so there's a lot to see and do. Taking in even a representative sample involves at least a month and going to many destinations, although this is feasible. The most difficult question is 'where to start?'

If you are planning your first trip to the States, you may just want spend a couple of weeks in New York, Miami, San Francisco or one of the fabulous national parks. (A note about New York: the small island of Manhattan is untypical of the US in many ways. An important distinction for travelers is the use of the car. Almost indispensable anywhere else in the States, a car is just a burden in New York. Taxis, buses, and the subway are simple and efficient, and besides, parking is a nightmare.)

For cross-country trips, Greyhound buses reach all over the continent. Trains are less practical, except along the East, Southern, or West coasts. Flying is often the best choice for long distances. On the 'shuttles' between New York and Washington or Boston, taking

Key composer

America's *Star Spangled Banner*, the national anthem, was written by composer Francis Scott Key in 1814.

Fun on the ice at Millennium Park, Chicago

a plane is like taking a bus. But do try a bus or a car if you can: it's the best way to get a taste of the country's immensity and the American romance of the road.

From New York, the most convenient regions to include in a short stay are the Mid-Atlantic (Washington, DC and Philadelphia) for the historically minded, and/or New England (Boston and the resorts in Massachusetts and Connecticut) for anyone who would like to mix history with relaxation. Or there's Florida and the Gulf Coast in the South for those who want nothing but fun on the endless beaches, or at Orlando's Walt Disney World Resort and other theme parks.

Another possibility for a two-week vacation is to combine New York with an excursion farther afield, either clear across the continent to California, or to one of the country's natural wonders such as the Grand Canyon or Yellowstone. New York, especially in summer, is an exhilarating but exhausting experience, so you'll need to pace yourself for the rest of the trip.

A Longer Stay

For a month-long stay, your itinerary might include New York-Boston-Washington, then directly to California, making your way back East via Yellowstone or the Grand Canyon, perhaps taking in San Antonio or Santa Fe for a taste of Southwestern America, followed by a distinctive big city like New Orleans or Chicago. Then finish up with a rest on a beach in Florida till your plane carries you home. If you want to see a lot of America in your four weeks, resist the temptation to start with California; you may be so seduced that you'll forget to look at the rest of the country.

The combinations are endless, but remember that Americans themselves like the good life to be both exciting and relaxed. If you want to survive your vacation, follow their example of enjoying both the big city *and* the parks or resorts. Even a town like Chicago has sandy beaches on the lake; New Orleans has its restful bayou country; New York has Long Island; Boston has Cape Cod; and there are beaches near much of Los Angeles.

NEW YORK CITY   HABIBIS

Perhaps more than any other place on earth, New York is a city people feel they know before they arrive. Films and photographs have so stamped it into the popular consciousness that you believe that you're already familiar with the gigantic chasms of skyscrapers, the underworld steam puffing through the manhole covers, and the milling crowds of people.

Then, one day, you go. And it's more than you ever dreamed. Coming into Manhattan from JFK airport, the city's skyscrapers loom higher, more impressive than in any movie. In the flesh, the crowds on Madison and Fifth avenues are a drama of color impossible to conceive of in the abstract. Right in there among the city's Irish, Italians, Chinese, Jews, Germans, Puerto Ricans, and African-Americans, not to forget the white Anglo-Saxon Protestants, you'll plunge into a unique travel adventure. Most other places have been discovered; New York is new every time.

The Brooklyn Bridge and Lower Manhattan skyline

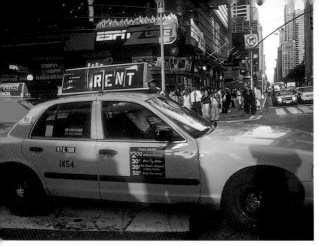

New York taxis are a good way to get around

While you can't know America without seeing New York, don't mistake it for the rest of the US. No other city has a more diverse population. Founded as New Amsterdam by the Dutch in 1626, the city numbered 1,500 inhabitants speaking 18 languages by 1644. Today more than 300 languages are spoken among the city's 8 million residents. While the terrorist attack of September 11, 2001, on the World Trade Center forever altered the face – and mindset – of New York, it did not diminish the spirit of the 'greatest city in the world.'

The Island of Manhattan

This island, 13 miles (21km) long and 2 miles (3km) wide, encompasses almost everything you will want to see. The other four boroughs, Brooklyn, Queens, Staten Island, and The Bronx – all mostly residential – have their own special flavors, but for locals and tourists, Manhattan *is* New York.

Manhattan is an easy place to find your way around. It divides simply into three basic parts: Uptown, Midtown, and Downtown (which, unlike other American cities, is the lower rather than the central part of town). Uptown is north of 59th Street, Midtown speaks for itself, and Downtown is the area south of 34th Street.

The backbone of the island is Fifth Avenue; all areas to the west of it as far as the Hudson are known as the West Side, while the East Side covers the area between Fifth Avenue and the East River. Fifth Avenue begins at Washington Square down in Greenwich Village.

There and in the Wall Street area, streets still have the names and irregular lines of the colonial era. Otherwise, all the roads intersect at right angles and the streets have numbers rather than names. The avenues (First to Twelfth) run north–south, and streets (1st to 220th) run east–west. Some avenues have names – York, Lexington, Madison, and Park. (Attempts to rename Sixth the 'Avenue of the Americas' have always seemed doomed.) Broadway, obeying no rules, runs more or less diagonally.

With the grid system of rectangular blocks, New Yorkers will pinpoint a place not by street number but by the nearest inter-section of street and avenue; e.g., the Whitney Museum is at Madison and 75th, one block east and seven blocks south of the Metropolitan (Fifth and 82nd). This is the only form of location that a New York cabbie will accept for any location other than a major landmark.

Washington Square

Midtown
Your hotel may well be located in Midtown, so it's easy to cover the area on foot. One of New York's many distinctions is that it's a great city for walking; sidewalks are wide and the crowds are always in-teresting. At any rate, the cen-ter is the place to begin.

Rockefeller Center: This soaring cluster of Indiana limestone towers between Fifth and Sixth avenues, from 48th to 51st streets, is the magnetic core of New York City. John D. Rockefeller, Jr leased the site from Columbia University in 1928 to rescue it from the infamy of Prohibition speakeasy saloons. These quickly disappeared under the first skyscrapers of a booming business and communications center, linked by an underground pedestrian concourse, which includes over 200 stores and restaurants.

You immediately sense the cheerful genius of the place with the fountains and flower beds of the **Channel Gardens** that slope down from Fifth Avenue south of 50th Street to the sunken plaza. With a nod to the English Channel, the gardens separate the Maison Française on the left and the British Empire Building on the right. At the end is **Rockefeller Plaza**, parasoled garden café in summer and ice-skating rink in winter. Watched over by a statue of Prometheus, the plaza is dominated by the center's tallest tower, the **GE Building**, home of NBC Television. The best way to see all that Rockefeller Center has to offer is to take one of the organized tours. The tours last one hour and fifteen minutes,

New York's Best Bridges

Water-laced New York has 65 bridges to hold it together, 14 of them connecting to Manhattan Island. The 1,595ft (486m) Brooklyn Bridge created a sensation when it opened in 1883, but was plagued by misfortune from the start. Its engineer, John Roebling, died in the early phases of the project as a result of an accident. His son carried on and was paralysed during the job. Nonetheless, the bridge, with its wire webbing, is a beautiful success. It is illuminated at night, offering great views. The 3,500ft (1,067m) George Washington Bridge spans the Hudson between Manhattan and New Jersey. The Manhattan Bridge has spawned an artists' community called Down Under the Manhattan Bridge Overpass (DUMBO). Newest is the 4,260ft (1,298m) Verrazano-Narrows Bridge from Brooklyn to Staten Island, which opened in 1964.

Radio City Music Hall was built in the 1930s

and there's at least one departing every hour the center is open, which is every day except Thanksgiving and Christmas.

At one time, Rockefeller Center was supposed to be built around a new Metropolitan Opera House. Instead, they built **Radio City Music Hall** (tel: 212-247-4777; www.radiocity.com), on the corner of Sixth Avenue and 50th Street. Radio City is one of the world's most marvellous movie theater-cum-variety palaces – a brilliant 1930s pick-me-up for the Depression blues.

Try to see a show here with the Rockettes, America's most famous troupe of dancing girls, kicking their legs to Radio City's own symphony orchestra and wonderful Wurlitzer organ, the world's biggest. At the very least, take one of the backstage tours organized seven days a week. The shimmering chandeliers and mirrors of the lobby would have impressed King Louis XIV. The auditorium, seating over 6,000, is ornamented with fantastic semicircular bands of light. It's hard to imagine that they nearly tore it down in the 1970s, but, as the *New York Times* said in support of the public outcry, 'If Radio City Music Hall really closes, it will be a little like closing New York.' Thankfully, they kept both open.

Another of Rockefeller Center's major attractions is the **Top of the Rock** (tel: 212-698-2000; www.topoftherocknyc.com; open until midnight). Situated 70 floors above ground, the deck offers a different perspective of the city to the Empire State, including terrific views of Central Park and the Empire State itself.

Fifth Avenue: This boulevard – at least the stretch between 34th Street and Central Park – is synonymous with luxury, to sample or to observe. If your budget won't stretch to a stay at the Plaza Hotel, you can bask in the understated opulence of the diamond-studded windows of Tiffany's, or Cartier's, or Arpels & Van Cleef. These are fantastic, especially at Christmastime. Or stroll around the smart department stores like Saks Fifth Avenue, Bergdorf Goodman, or Henri Bendel. For a touch of foreign flair, try the stylish high fashion of French and Italian boutiques like Gucci that take advantage of New York and the sophistication of New York shoppers.

A Fifth Avenue triumph is **Trump Tower** at 56th Street. Inside you will find the ultimate atrium, a cool, airy space six stories high, finished in rich rose-colored marble and gleaming brass.

Amid all this sometimes overripe elegance, turn off a moment at West 47th Street – '**Diamond Row**,' center of the diamond trade, where black-coated Hasidic Jews from Eastern Europe hurry back and forth with a glitter in their paper bags, under the benign protection of uniformed and plainclothes police.

The valiant effort of **St Patrick's Cathedral** (between 50th and 51st) to imitate Cologne's Gothic cathedral in Germany is a little lost today among the skyscrapers of Rockefeller Center and the Olympic Tower next door. But the 1879 building comes into its own on the occasion of the Irish-Catholic parade on St Patrick's Day (March 17), when the Cardinal greets the marchers.

Times Square and Broadway: The *New York Times* purports to publish 'All the News That's Fit to Print,' and the newspaper's Times Tower gave its name to that bizarre mixture of chic and sleaze – Times Square (on the north side of 42nd Street between Broadway and Seventh Avenue). Times Square in fact encompasses the area from 42nd to 47th Street, between Sixth and Eighth avenues. The heart of the theater district, it was also headquarters for the city's seediest strip joints and sex shops. Excellent restaurants rubbed shoulders with the seamiest bars. Sleek limousines deposited ladies in evening dress, just down the street from prostitutes, drunks, and dope-dealers, all serenaded by street-entertainers similarly varying from the sophisticated talents of an out-of-work jazz musician to the crummy twanging of someone who stole a guitar.

But today, thanks to former mayor Rudolph Giuliani and committed community involvement, Times Square has undergone a major facelift. To the dismay of some and the relief of others, Disney is the anchor of this renovation, its presence towering over the corner of 42nd and Seventh. But now entire blocks have been redone. Old theaters that once showed horror and pornographic movies have been restored to their original

St Patrick's Cathedral reflected

beauty and purpose: legitimate theater. The headquarters of NASDAQ, Virgin Records, and other shiny stores have replaced drugs and pornography, and the new neon lights expand the Broadway area known as 'the Great White Way.'

If the Times Square/Broadway atmosphere gets to be too much for you, relax in the snug lobby or the Blue Bar of the **Algonquin Hotel**, one of the greatest monuments of Manhattan's 1920s literary scene (44th Street, between Fifth and Sixth avenues).

42nd Street: Another haven of peace, as well as an architectural delight, is the **New York Public Library** (Fifth Avenue between 40th and 42nd; tel: 212-930-0830; www.nypl.com). The building is a masterpiece of Beaux-Arts, a 1911 American reinterpretation of the French design school's neoclassical style at its restrained best. Set back at the end of a wide stairway, the facade's three arches with coupled Corinthian columns around the entrance invite you in off the street for an hour's tranquility. In this most public of public libraries, relax with a book in the great reading room, admire the changing exhibitions in Gottesman Hall, or laze outside on the steps, where you are well protected by sculptor E.C. Potter's giant stone lions.

East on 42nd Street, at the south end of Park Avenue, **Grand Central Terminal**, terminus of the Vanderbilt railroad empire, is as much a legend as it is a building. Like the library, its Beaux-Arts pedigree is impeccable (although it took a US Supreme Court decision to save it from destruction). Over the great clock of the facade, the sculpture of the eagle among standing and reclining Roman deities apparently symbolizes America's special relationship with the gods. Completed in 1920, the station's 123 tracks built on two levels, 66 above and 57 below, move half a million people in and out of the city every day. Watch them at rush hour in the vast barrel-vaulted main concourse, which has now been restored to its original splendor.

The **Met Life Building** over the station infuriated art critics at the time, but the neighborhood has some other impressive skyscrapers. A wonderful example of Art Deco can be seen in the stainless-steel swordfish pinnacle of the **Chrysler Building** (Lexington Avenue and 42nd Street). Of course, its glazed enamel, white-brick, and stainless-steel silhouette is best seen glinting in the sunlight from a distance, but from the upper floors of nearby hotels you get a close-up of the weird gargoyles inspired by various radiator caps for Chrysler cars.

Be sure to take a look at the lobby inside the building, which, with its dark- and light-wood interior, is a near-perfect example of the stylish Art Deco form that swept the world in the 1920s and '30s.

The Chrysler Building

CitiGroup Center (Lexington Avenue between 53rd and 54th) brings an outstanding touch to the skyline with its dramatically sloping silver roof. At ground level, its urban consciousness is emphasized by a lively three-story 'market' of stores and restaurants around a skylit central courtyard. By the same architect, Hugh Stubbins, is free-standing, polygonal **St Peter's Lutheran Church** (42nd Street and Lexington Avenue), with a lovely chapel decorated by sculptor Louise Nevelson.

Arguably the best of the sleek office blocks on Park Avenue is the **Seagram Building** (between 52nd and 53rd). Designed by Mies van der Rohe and Philip Johnson, the pure lines of this bronze-tinted glass skyscraper are considered the ultimate refinement of Mies's International Style. Inside is the Four Seasons restaurant and Picasso's stage backdrop for *Le Tricorne*.

Taking in the view from the
Empire State Building

The United Nations (First Avenue, between 42nd and 48th; tel: 212-963-8687; www.un.org; tours daily): John D. Rockefeller, Jr donated the 18-acre (7-hectare) site to persuade UN members to make their headquarters in New York.

A team of international architects, led by American Wallace K. Harrison and including the Swiss-French master Le Corbusier, managed to put up buildings in the early 1950s with considerably more unity and harmony than the diplomats ever achieved inside. The headquarters consist of four main buildings: the 39-floor Secretariat Building; the General Assembly Building (the lower block with the concave roof); the Conference Building; and the Dag Hammarskjöld Library, memorial to the late secretary-general, which was added in 1961. The complex is best seen from the East River on a boat ride around Manhattan.

At the information desk in the lobby (45th and First), you can arrange to take a guided tour of the whole UN complex. Member states have donated parts of the complex – the three Council Rooms, for instance, were the gifts of Norway, Denmark, and Sweden, while Great Britain provided the Barbara Hepworth Sculpture in the plaza pool (the pool itself was a donation from American schoolchildren).

For a pleasant view of the skyscrapers along UN Plaza, buy a sandwich to eat in the garden, or have your lunch in the Delegates' Dining Room overlooking the East River (passholders only; check about reservations at the lobby information desk). You can get reasonably priced crafts from all over the world at the gift shop. The post office here sells UN stamps only (not American) for letters and cards posted inside the complex.

➤ **Empire State Building** (corner of Fifth Avenue and 34th Street; tel: 212-736-3100; www.esbnyc.com; open until 2am): Everything about the Empire State Building is huge: 102 stories; 60,000 tons of steel; 3,500 miles (5,670km) of telephone wires and cables; 60 miles (97km) of pipes; the building occupies 1½ million cubic yards (1 million cubic meters), and King Kong had to climb 1,472ft (449m). Built in 1931, most of the building's office space was empty in the early Depression years, and it paid its taxes with income from sightseers.

To get your ticket to the **Observation Deck**, go down to the basement – arrows point the way. The elevator takes you to the 80th floor, where you catch the 'local' to the 86th. The outside platform offers a fantastic view, often of ships 40 miles (65km) out at sea, or in winter you may choose to remain inside the heated shelter for protection from the elements. There is also a third elevator that goes to an observation deck on the 102nd floor, but this is sometimes closed. The deck stands at the base of a 204ft (62m) high communications tower and antenna, from which TV and FM radio stations transmit programs to the metropolitan area. One of the most exciting aspects is the way the building changes color depending on the occasion: turning green for St Patrick's Day, or red, white, and blue for the Fourth of July. For a complete list of lighting schedules and the occasions they represent, consult the website.

The Empire State Building

Downstairs again on 34th Street, you're in a popular shopping area. Check out **Macy's**, or stroll over to 32nd and Seventh Avenue, where you'll see the entertainment and sports venue **Madison Square Garden** (4 Pennsylvania Plaza; tel: 212-465-6741; www.madisonsquaregarden.com; tours daily) which claims to be the 'world's most famous arena.'

Downtown

Wall Street Area: Here, at the southern end of Manhattan, the skyscrapers close in on each other across narrow canyons to form ramparts for this almost awe-inspiring capital of capitalism, known as Wall Street. Appropriately, the wall was conceived in 1653 as a protection for America's first great financial bargain – a wooden stockade to keep the Indians from invading the settlement on the island they had sold to the Dutch for the legendary price of $24 (60 guilders) 30 years earlier. Today, few addresses anywhere hold greater prestige.

The New York Stock Exchange

The beating heart of the Financial District is the **New York Stock Exchange**, reverentially designed as a Roman temple. Unfortunately, the viewing platform to the excitement of the trading floor is no longer open to the public.

From the exotic temple of the moneylenders it's but a short step to **Trinity Church** (which dates from 1846) at the Broadway end of Wall Street. This, the first of America's

Gothic Revival churches, offers tired office workers –
and weary sightseers – a few
moments' rest and peace in
the tranquil cemetery garden.
Alexander Hamilton, the first
Secretary of the Treasury, is
buried here.

During the brief period
that New York was the United
States' first capital, **Federal
Hall** (corner of Wall and Nas-
sau streets, demolished in 1812

Fraunces Tavern

and rebuilt in 1842) was the home of Congress and the place
where George Washington took the oath as president on April
30, 1789. His bronze statue stands outside. The other landmark
dating from the inception of the Republic is **Fraunces Tavern**,
located at the corner of Pearl and Broad streets. It was here that
Washington took leave of his officers at the end of the Revolutionary War, six years before his inauguration. The tavern owner,
Samuel Fraunces, later became Washington's steward in the White
House. The present building is an approximate reconstruction of
the original. Downstairs is a restaurant, while upstairs is a museum. Among the exhibits is a lock of Washington's hair.

World Trade Center Site: To the north of Trinity Church, the
Twin Towers of the World Trade Center soared skyward until September 11, 2001. On an exceptionally clear and calm morning,
two hijacked US passenger jets, under the control of terrorists,
struck the towers in rapid succession and brought them down.
The towers, which at 110 stories were the tallest buildings in the
world at the time of their completion in 1973 and remained the
tallest buildings in New York until their collapse, were totally destroyed in the attack. Around 3,000 people, many of them police-
men and firemen, perished in the catastrophe, amounting to the

Lady Liberty greets the masses

greatest single-day loss of human life in the US since the Battle of Antietam in the Civil War. A period of both public and private mourning ensued, culminating in a staged competition open to architects around the world to come up with an appropriate replacement.

The building selected was Daniel Libeskind's Freedom Tower. When completed, it will rise 1,776ft (541m) into the air, and will once again be the tallest in the world. The **Tribute WTC Visitor Center** (120 Liberty Street; tel: 866-737-1184; www.tributewtc.org), made up of five themed galleries, is very moving; a rolling list of names reminds of the scale of the loss, while personal photographs celebrate the victims' lives. Other nearby memorials include **St Paul's Chapel**, which has a permanent display, and the *Icon of Hope* in Battery Park, a global sphere that was pulled from the wreckage of the towers.

Statue of Liberty (15-minute ferry ride from Battery Park; tel: 212-363-3200; www.nps.gov/stli): It is difficult to imagine a more eloquent symbol than the message of the 'Lady' of the Statue of Liberty offered those desperate refugees sailing to the New World at the end of the 19th century. Today, few Americans or foreigners, however cynical, can remain totally blasé about this monument, rising 305ft (93m) from its pedestal base to the tip of the torch. The statue, built by French sculptor Auguste Bartholdi and structural engineer Gustave Eiffel, was a gift from the people of France, presented on July 4, 1884, and erected here in 1886. The statue's full name is 'Liberty Illuminating the World,' a French idea linking the French and American revolutions. The $250,000 it cost was jointly and privately funded, with the French paying for the statue and the Americans for the pedestal. Visitors climb the steps to the pedestal, where a glass ceiling provides a view into the intricate interior structure. Timed passes eliminate extremely long waits.

West of Liberty Island is **Ellis Island**, where 12 million of those 'huddled masses' passed through immigration checks between 1892 and 1924. The medically suspect were marked with chalk on their lapels – H for heart, K for hernia, Sc for scalp, X for mental defects. Today, the 'island of tears' has been declared a national monument and the old immigration station restored and turned into the **American Museum of Immigration**, which tells the often wretched stories of the millions who passed through here.

If you don't want to join the crowds on Liberty Island, but would like to take a cooling boat ride with a marvelous view of Manhattan, take the **Staten Island Ferry** (also from Battery Park, tel: 212-269-5755). It's the best bargain ride in town: passengers travel for free. For a superior view, stand forward on the second deck.

Invitation to Hope

Symbolically, the Statue of Liberty was the first sight of the new world for many millions of immigrants arriving by boat over the last two centuries.

The famous inscription on the pedestal of the Statue of Liberty was written by Emma Lazarus, a New York poet, in response to the Russian pogroms of the 1880s which drove so many Jews to cross the Atlantic.

Her lines have since taken on a universal significance, and shone as a beacon of hope for all the world's oppressed:

'Give me your tired, your poor,
Your huddled masses yearning to breathe free,
The wretched refuse of your teeming shore.
Send these, the homeless, tempest-tossed, to me:
I lift my lamp beside the golden door.'

Lower East Side: The area from Canal Street north to Houston is where the immigrants first headed. Most stayed just long enough to learn English and then headed Uptown or beyond the Hudson River. Chinese, Jews, and Italians chose to settle here a little longer in their own enclaves. The Chinese are still here in strength, and although the area is becoming increasingly trendy – full of boutiques and hot music clubs – the colors, sounds, and smells of the other communities also linger on vividly enough for you to capture, in an easy afternoon's stroll, the old flavor.

If you take the East Side subway to **Chinatown**, you won't go wrong: the Canal Street station has signs in both Roman and Chinese characters. The telephone booths have pagoda roofs, stores sell jade jewelry, grocers display snow peas and winter melon, and countless restaurants vie for attention with their Cantonese, Shanghainese, and Szechwan specialties.

A Lower East Side tenement

Well over 100,000 Chinese live in Chinatown, a loosely defined area centered around Canal Street, Mott Street, and Chatham Square. The earliest arrivals came to the country during the California Gold Rush in the 19th century; most of the immigrants today come directly from Hong Kong. To learn about the area, visit the **Museum of Chinese in the Americas** (70 Mulberry Street; tel: 212-619-4785; www.moca-nyc.org).

Many Chinese from the rest of New York (and even from other parts of the state) come here on weekends to do their grocery shopping and to enjoy a meal out. Supermarkets sell the finest China teas, and pretty porcelain to drink them from. Take a look at the **Buddhist Temple** (64 Mott Street), where you can purchase your fortune for a small sum.

South of Mott Street, at 55 St James Place, is the city's oldest 'monument,' the Shearith Israel cemetery, founded in 1683 by Portuguese Sephardic Jews

Exotic Chinatown produce

from Brazil. Manhattan's Jewish Quarter, settled principally by Eastern European Ashkenazi Jews, is on the northeast side of Chinatown, around the old Hester Street market. The **Lower East Side Tenement Museum** (108 Orchard Street; tel: 212-431-0233; www.tenement.org) is dedicated to the lives of desperately poor 19th-century immigrants. The visitors' center is the starting point for tours of the tenements, which can only be visited with a guide. Afterwards, try a pastrami (seasoned smoked beef) sandwich and a cup of lemon tea in one of the kosher restaurants.

Even tinier than its name suggests, **Little Italy** is centered on Mulberry Street a few blocks to the northwest – and shares its southern part with Chinatown. The Italian section is now principally a gastronomic hub, with expensive as well as moderately priced restaurants and espresso bars, high-quality caterers, and, scattered among them, souvenir shops and the occasional grocery store specializing in scrumptious homemade and imported Italian delicacies. The street is at its liveliest during the 10-day Feast of San Gennaro in September: be sure to come with a good appetite.

Greenwich Village and SoHo: The village was once New York's artistic center, home of writers such as Mark Twain, Edith

Summer in the city

Washington Square, at the south end of Fifth Avenue, is where locals congregate during the long, hot summer months.

Wharton, and O. Henry, and painters like Edward Hopper, Ben Shahn, and Franz Kline. In the 1950s, villagers swayed to the jazz of Miles Davis and Bill Evans at the Village Vanguard; in the 1960s they heard the first jokes of Woody Allen at the Bitter End Café. The venerable and lively **Village Vanguard** (178 Seventh Avenue South, tel: 212- 255-4037) still sports a fine jazz roster.

At night the jazz cellars are as aromatic as ever, and a few coffee houses remain. A bygone charm can still be found in **MacDougal Alley** and **Washington Mews**, while the hottest trends and coolest restaurants in town can be sampled in the former butcher shops of the **Meatpacking District**, the northwestern part of the village.

Henry James lived for a few months on **Washington Square**, the title of one of his novels and heart of the New York University campus. His grandmother lived in one of the Greek Revival houses along the north side (No. 19). Look up and enjoy this stretch of Fifth Avenue from **Washington Arch**, the work of the architect Stanford White, commissioned in 1889 to mark the centenary of George Washington's inauguration as president.

In the 1970s the area south of West Houston Street, **SoHo** (short for **So**uth of **Ho**uston), followed the pattern of Greenwich Village. Artists who couldn't afford the rents after the village's commercialization moved south to the abandoned lofts and warehouse floors of this industrial district. With the success of the avant-garde galleries on West Broadway, especially No. 420, where Pop Art's Andy Warhol, Robert Rauschenberg, and Roy Lichtenstein displayed their works, rents soared. The interior decorators and restaurateurs took over from the artists, many of whom moved out, first heading southwest to **TriBeCa** (**Tri**angle **Be**low **Ca**nal, now a fun, hip place to go shopping or eat out), later to Chelsea, and, finally, to the borough of Queens.

Upper West Side, Central Park, and Uptown

The Upper West Side: Much has changed in this neighborhood west of Central Park. The area bordering the park has always been prosperous, with fine and famous apartment buildings like **The Dakota,** former home of John Lennon and the film set for the brilliant but creepy movie *Rosemary's Baby*. But in the last decade 'new money' has arrived, and along with it soaring, signature buildings like the **Trump International Hotel and Tower**, the gleaming towers of the **Time Warner Center** (where you can take the CNN Studio Tour; tel: 866-426-6692), and the shimmering, ceramic premises of the **Museum of Arts and Design** (2 Columbus Circle; tel: 212-299-7777; www.madmuseum.org).

One mainstay of the Upper West Side is the **Lincoln Center** (West 62nd to 66th, between Columbus and Amsterdam; www.lincolncenter.org; one-hour guided tours start at the 'Met'). With most of the prestigious fine-arts museums located on the affluent Upper East Side, the Lincoln Center for the Performing Arts

The Lincoln Center for the Performing Arts

Neighborhoods

New Yorkers are fond of their abbreviations. As well as SoHo and TriBeCa, NoHo means North of Houston and NoLita stands for 'North of Little Italy,' even though it is geographically incorrect.

provided a good balance and a perfect fillip for the revival of the neighborhood in the 1960s. Since his father had to shelve his plan to put the Metropolitan Opera in Rockefeller Center, John D. Rockefeller III led the drive to find it another home, along with the New York Philharmonic, the New York City Ballet, and the Juilliard School of Music.

As you go up the steps to the plaza on Columbus Avenue – especially at night with the central fountain bathed in ethereal light – you may find the effect a little self-consciously 'prestigious.' But the buildings around the plaza are undoubtedly important, starting on the left with the modern classicism of Philip Johnson's **New York State Theater**, home of the New York City Ballet and New York City Opera. At the back of the plaza is Wallace K. Harrison's grand design for the **Metropolitan Opera House**, with its tall glass facade arched in travertine marble and red-carpeted lobby with dazzling Austrian crystal chandeliers. You can see the immense paintings by Marc Chagall from the plaza.

Originally completed in 1962, **Avery Fisher Hall** had to have its hall reconstructed several times over the next 14 years before achieving today's excellent acoustics and admired architectural simplicity. At the back of a handsome reflecting pool with sculpture by Henry Moore is the **Vivian Beaumont Theater**, originally intended as the base for a New York repertory company. Designed by Eero Saarinen, it houses a large round auditorium with a versatile movable stage at plaza level and the small Mitzi Newhouse Theater below.

A bridge across 65th Street connects Lincoln Center to the **Juilliard School**, a world-famous music conservatory. On the first floor, in Alice Tully Hall, if you're lucky, you can listen to chamber music ensembles and afternoon concerts by Juilliard students.

Central Park: A vast green breathing space in the center of Manhattan (⅔ mile/1km wide and 2½ miles/4km long), Central Park is a sports field, playground, and picnic spot for tens of thousands of city-dwellers. In the 1840s, the poet William Cullen Bryant realized that New York needed more parks for its rapidly expanding population. He launched a campaign to persuade the city to buy the land, which was at that time wasteland beyond the city limits. Landscape gardeners Frederick Law Olmsted and Calvert Vaux were called on to design the park, which took 3,000 workers 16 years to complete. Conceived in the English style, the park doesn't really look manmade – the lake, the 'forests,' the paths, and the meadows seem to have been there forever. By day it's perfectly safe to walk in the park, but avoid it at night, unless you're going with a group to the summer theater or music events.

Walkers in the park

Starting from the southeast corner of the park, skirt the pond to the small, modern **zoo**. Then stop in at The Dairy, which is the **Central Park Visitors' Center**, for a calendar of park events. From here, head up the wide, tree-lined Mall to the ornamented **Bethesda Fountain and Terrace**. In summer, you can rent a rowboat at the Loeb boathouse – to your right – for a trip on the pretty lake stretching out below the terrace. To the east, at the oval **Conservatory Water**, permit holders sail their miniature boats next to statues of Hans Christian Andersen and Alice in Wonderland. On a hill level with the Metropolitan Museum of Art stands **Cleopatra's Needle**, a 3,000-year-old obelisk that was a gift from Egypt in the late 19th century. A more recent addition to the park is **Strawberry Fields** (Central Park West between West 71st and 74th streets), Yoko Ono's horticultural memorial to her husband, John Lennon, who was murdered in 1980 across the street, in front of The Dakota.

The 1½-mile (2.5km) path around the **Reservoir** is popular with joggers. Sports are played in the park every day, but most of all on Sundays in the summer. There are miles of bicycle and jogging paths, which are turned into cross-country ski runs in winter, along with tennis courts, an ice-skating rink, and playgrounds.

Free open-air concerts and operas are presented on the **Great Lawn** during the summer months, and in **Belvedere Castle** there are exhibits and special events. The **Delacorte Theatre**, south of 81st Street on the west side of the park, is the venue for the Shakespeare in the Park Festival (free; line up ahead of time for tickets).

Harlem: Harlem, the cradle of African-American culture, has undergone a second renaissance in recent years, marked by the arrival of former president Bill Clinton, who established an office here in 2001. Harlem's main thoroughfares bustle with shoppers choosing among well-known mall retailers, local merchants, and street vendors, some of them offering exotic wares. A drive through Harlem is included in many sightseeing tours of Manhattan, and a number of local agencies offer jazz and gospel tours. (For tour bookings, contact NYC & Company; http://nycgo.com). Important museums include the **Schomburg Center for Research in Black Culture** (515 Malcolm X Boulevard; tel: 212-491-2200; www.nypl.org/research/sc) and the **Studio Museum** (144 West 125th Street; tel: 212-864-4500; www.studiomuseum.org).

Harlem stretches from the northern reaches of Central Park to 178th Street. In the 1950s, it was the home of a million African-Americans from the southern states and the Caribbean. Today barely a quarter of a million remain. Optimists attribute this exodus to the housing programs and improvements in living standards. Pessimists say that dilapidation just drove people out to ghettos such as the South Bronx.

Founded by Dutch settlers, Harlem remained a village separate from the rest of Manhattan until the end of the 19th century, when middle-class Americans moved north away from the new immigrants of the Lower East Side. African-Americans started moving in around 1920, the beginning of the Jazz Age. Leaving the cotton fields of the South, for them New York was the 'Promised Land.' Duke Ellington and Cab Calloway played the Cotton Club and the Savoy, drawing

One of Harlem's many churches

crowds of white people Uptown, where, during Prohibition, alcohol was easier to obtain. Now emerging from the crime-ridden doldrums, renewal is spreading. There's jazz at the **Lenox Lounge** (288 Lenox Avenue at 125th Street) and **Showmans** (375 125th Street), soul food at **Sylvia's** (328 Malcolm X Boulevard), and variety entertainment at the resurrected **Apollo Theater** (253 West 125th Street), where Amateur Night reigns on Wednesday evenings.

Around **Edgecombe Avenue** the architecture becomes quite impressive. One of New York's last remnants of colonial architecture is the **Morris-Jumel Mansion** (Edgecombe at West 160th Street, tel: 212-923-8008; www.morrisjumel.org), a stately house set in a picturesque garden. Built in 1765 and used as a headquarters by George Washington at the beginning of the Revolutionary War, it was bought in 1810 by a French wine merchant,

Stephen Jumel. Jumel's widow, Eliza, a remarkable woman who claimed to have slept with both George Washington and Napoleon, married her second husband, Aaron Burr (third vice-president of the US), here. Now it is a museum of American decorative arts from the 18th and 19th centuries.

Also worth the trek to northern Manhattan is **The Cloisters** (Fort Tryon Park at 190th Street; tel: 212-923-3700; www.met museum.org), a tranquil spot that showcases the Metropolitan Museum's collection of medieval art. French and Spanish monastic cloisters, Gothic chapels and a 12th-century chapterhouse were shipped from Europe and reassembled here.

The east side of Harlem is a mainly Puerto Rican community also known as **Spanish Harlem**. Visit **El Museo del Barrio** (Fifth Avenue at 104th Street; tel: 212-831-7272; www.el museo.org), a museum devoted to the art and culture of Latin America. In the summer months, take in the lively atmosphere of **La Marqueta**, a market on Park Avenue.

Metropolitan Museum of Art

Museums in New York City

With 120 museums, it would be easy to spend the rest of your life in a New York cultural palace. Here is just a small selection:

Metropolitan Museum of Art (Fifth Avenue at 82nd Street; tel: 212-535-7710; www.metmuseum.org): One of the world's great museums, the Metropolitan consists of nearly 250 rooms with over 4,500 paintings and drawings, 1 million prints, 4,000 musical instruments, and countless pieces of furniture and sculpture. Only a quarter of the collection is on display at any one time. Especially interesting are the American Wing, a celebration of the architecture, decorative arts, and fine arts of the US; the Lehman collection of early Italian and French Impressionist painting; the primitive art in the Michael C. Rockefeller wing; the sections devoted to European painting from the 15th to the 20th centuries; the Islamic art section; the extensive Egyptian department; and the Greek and Roman galleries.

Museum of Modern Art (West 53rd Street between Fifth and Sixth avenues; tel: 212-708 9400; www.moma.org): MoMA to habitués, this fantastic museum boosted by the Rockefeller family has more than 100,000 works of art from 1880 to the present. An ambitious and highly successful 'refit' in 2004 virtually doubled the exhibition space, the better to see MoMA's breathtaking collections, which include Vincent Van Gogh's *The Starry Night* and Pablo Picasso's *Les Demoiselles d'Avignon*.

Guggenheim Museum (Fifth Avenue and 89th Street; tel: 212-423 3500; www.guggenheim.org): Designed by Frank Lloyd Wright, the museum's architecture is almost as important as its contents: late 19th- and 20th-century collections as well as works by Paul Klee, Kandinsky, and Chagall. The annex offers fine Van Gogh, Gauguin, and Modigliani paintings and a wonderful group of Picassos.

Whitney Museum of American Art (Madison Avenue and 75th Street; tel: 212-570-3676; www.whitney.org): Drawing on the great vigor of American 20th-century art, the museum has marvelously lit, imaginative, and adventurous exhibitions.

Frick Collection (70th Street and Fifth Avenue; tel. 212-288-0700; www.frick.org): Industrialist Henry Clay Frick's classical European paintings, furnishings, and other treasures are presented in the opulent and intimate setting of his own home.

American Museum of Natural History (Central Park West at 79th Street; tel: 212-769-5100; www.amnh.org): Renowned for its remarkable collection of dinosaur skeletons, it also has a planetarium, striking zoological dioramas and important anthropological exhibitions.

Cooper-Hewitt Museum (Fifth Avenue and 91st Street; tel: 212-849-8400; www.cooperhewitt.org): America's largest collection of decorative art from the 15th to the 20th centuries.

Museum of Jewish Heritage – A Living Memorial to the Holocaust (36 Battery Place, Battery Park City; tel: 1-646-437-4200; www.mjhnyc.org): Dedicated to 20th-century Jewish art and recollections of Holocaust survivors.

National Museum of the American Indian (1 Bowling Green, State and Whitehall streets; tel 212-514-3700; www.nmai.si.edu): Operated by the Smithsonian Institute, this free museum displays a collection of Native American art and artifacts in the historic Custom House.

Museum of the City of New York (Fifth Avenue and 103rd Street; tel: 212-534-1672; www.mcny.org): Important for the town's exciting history. Great old toys.

Intrepid Sea, Air & Space Museum (Pier 86, 46th Street and 12th Avenue; tel: 212-245-0072; www.intrepidmuseum.org): Centered on the converted World War II aircraft carrier *Intrepid*, with planes on the deck (including *Concorde*) and displays below. It's better than ever following a two-year renovation.

Excursions from New York City

Atlantic City (*NEW JERSEY*): (*From New York, Lincoln Tunnel and south via the Garden State Parkway*) Atlantic City has made its way into most American homes via the street names in the American version of Monopoly. But from around 1900 until

World War II, it was a major northeast entertainment center, featuring the likes of Benny Goodman, Duke Ellington, and, later, Frank Sinatra. It went into serious decline beginning in the 1950s, until gambling brought it back to life in the 1970s. The casinos are now its main attraction, although the quaint charm has not entirely disappeared from the painted facades of the stores along the 6-mile (10km) long **Boardwalk**, still laden with amusements, tacky temptations and bargains. The sea breeze is always refreshing, especially accompanying a mouthful of Atlantic City's famous saltwater taffy.

Niagara Falls *(NEW YORK STATE)*: The most remarkable attraction in New York State is Niagara Falls (tel: 716-278-1796; www.niagara-usa.com), where nature still triumphs over commercialism. No amount of pushy peddlers or 'honeymoon motels' can diminish the spectacle of that mass of white water plunging nearly 200ft (60m) on its way from Lake Erie down toward Lake Ontario.

The thundering Niagara Falls

It's worth looking at the falls from more than one perspective. Make your first vantage point Goat Island, a nice mini-tram ride from Prospect Point. The island divides the Niagara River into the eastern **American Falls** – 182ft (55m) high and 1,076ft (323m) wide – and the western **Horseshoe (Canadian) Falls** – 176ft (54m) high and 2,100ft (640m) wide – with a smaller cascade known as **Bridal Veil** off to the side. On Goat Island, choose between a helicopter tour over the whole falls area or an elevator (sometimes closed) down to where the water crashes into the lower river bed.

Here you can walk behind the wall of cascading water and experience the cataract's overpowering roar. Tour operators provide protective clothing, but nothing is totally waterproof against Niagara. Cable-cars take you high above the rapids; three boats, all named *Maid of the Mist*, give a safe view from the river. More adventurous is the Jetboat trip through the rapids at the base of the falls. There are numerous observation towers, the best being on the Canadian side (foreign and American visitors should bring passports). The viewpoints of the Skylon and Minolta towers are respectively 770ft (235m) and 665ft (203m) above the falls.

At night the Horseshoe Falls gleam in multicolored illuminations with 4,000 million units of candlepower generated by the falls themselves. The United States and Canada have collaborated to exploit Niagara's tremendous power resources – 2,190,000 kilowatts on the American side and 1,775,000 kilowatts on the Canadian side. Four miles (6.5km) north on Route 104 is the interesting **Niagara Power Project** showing how this energy is harnessed. A geological museum in **Prospect Park** describes how rock erosion will completely flatten out the falls in the next 30,000 to 40,000 years.

You can make a side trip to **Buffalo**, a charming city with a lively cultural life. The Albright-Knox Art Gallery (1285 Elmwood Avenue) has some fine examples of American and European art of the 18th, 19th, and 20th centuries. The gallery is set in lovely **Delaware Park**, landscaped by Frederick Law Olmsted, which includes a zoo with some Buffalo buffalo. The Buffalo Philharmonic Orchestra gives concerts at the Kleinhans Music Hall.

NEW ENGLAND

From north to south, New England comprises six states – Maine, New Hampshire, Vermont, Massachusetts, Rhode Island, and Connecticut, with Massachusetts's Boston as the undisputed capital. Their combined area would scarcely cover just one state in the West, but their historical significance in the American Republic's beginnings and their present role in political and cultural life are essential to the United States.

Beyond the historic fascination of New England are the rugged coastline and little fishing ports from the Canadian border down to Boston. Far-

Boats in Massachusetts

ther south lie the glorious sandy beaches of Cape Cod, while inland are the rolling hills of the Massachusetts Berkshires, the White Mountains of New Hampshire, and the lovely woods that cover most of the New England landscape.

Spring and summer are delightful times in New England, but the trees claim a special short season to themselves in the place where the expression 'Indian summer' came into being. After the first cool spell in fall, there's a sudden new burst of sunshine, when warm days and cool evenings create a spectacular explosion of color in the leaves. Telephone state and local tourist offices to get up-to-the-minute information on where to see the best displays, which usually peak around mid-October. This is also a great time for country fairs, communal flea markets, garage sales *(see page 210)*, and pay-for-what-you-pick apples and pears in the orchards.

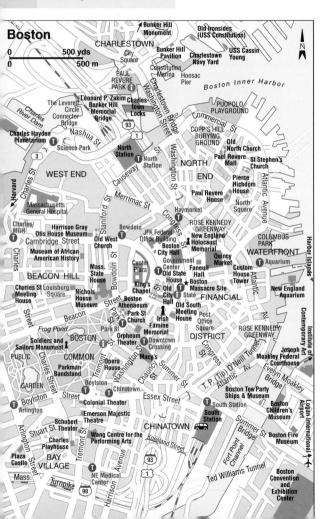

Boston

0 ___ 500 yds
0 ___ 500 m

CHARLESTOWN

Bunker Hill Monument
Old Ironsides (USS Constitution)
Bunker Hill Pavilion
Charlestown Navy Yard
USS Cassin Young
City Square
Charlestown Marina
Hoosac Pier
Boston Inner Harbor

PAUL REVERE PARK
Constitution

The Leverett Connector
Leonard P. Zakim Bunker Hill Memorial Bridge
Charlestown Bridge
Charles town Locks

PUOPOLO PLAYGROUND

Commercial St

Charles River Dam

Charles Hayden Planetarium
Science Park
Nashua St
North Station
North Station

COPP'S HILL BURYING GROUND
Old North Church
Paul Revere Mall
St Stephen's Church

WEST END

Washington Street
Causeway
Merrimac St

NORTH END

Pierce Hichdom House
Paul Revere House
North Square

Atlantic Avenue

Massachusetts General Hospital

Congress St

Haymarket

Charles/MGH
Harrison Gray Otis House Museum
Cambridge Street

Museum of African American History

Old West Church
Bowdoin
Staniford St

JFK Federal Office Building
Boston City Hall

ROSE KENNEDY GREENWAY
New England Holocaust Memorial

COLUMBUS PARK

WATERFRONT
Aquarium

Harbor Islands

BEACON HILL

Mass. State House
Bowdoin Street

Center Plaza
Government Center
Faneuil Hall

Quincy Market
Custom House Tower

Charles St Meeting House
Louisburg Square
Nichols House Museum

King's Chapel
Boston Athenaeum
Park St Church

Old State House
Boston Massacre Site
Old City Hall
State St
Old South Meeting House

FINANCIAL

New England Aquarium

Beacon Street

Frog Pond

Soldiers and Sailors Monument

BOSTON COMMON

Park Street

Orpheum Theater

Irish Famine Memorial

Post Office Square

DISTRICT

ROSE KENNEDY GREENWAY

Institute of Contemporary Art

PUBLIC

Parkman Bandstand

Opera House
Macy's
Downtown Crossing

Summer St

Congress St

Joseph Moakley Federal Courthouse

GARDEN

Boylston

Boylston Street

Macy's
Chauncy St

Summer St

Evelyn Moakley Bridge

Boston Tea Party Ships & Museum

Logan International Airport

Arlington
Boylston

Chinatown

Essex Street

T. P. (Tip) O'Neill Tunnel

Atlantic Av

South Station
South Station

Boston Children's Museum

Colonial Theater

Emerson Majestic Theatre

CHINATOWN

Fort Point Channel

Boston Fire Museum

Stuart St
Schubert Theater

Charles Playhouse

Wang Centre for the Performing Arts

Kneeland Street

Summer St

Tremont Street

Plaza Castle

BAY VILLAGE

Mass.

Turnpike

NE Medical Center

Ted Williams Tunnel

Boston Convention and Exhibition Center

Harrison Avenue

Boston (MASSACHUSETTS)

This city encompasses the essence of America's origins and the blossoming of its 20th century. It's a bustling place of 600,000 people inside the narrow city limits, but nearly 4 million if you include all the townships of metropolitan Boston.

Along with a huge student population, Boston houses the Anglo-Saxon descendants of the original settlers, the very proper 'Brahmins' in the elegant neighborhood of Beacon Hill. They now play a distinguished second fiddle to the Irish, who spread through the town after fleeing the 1845 potato famine, first as laborers, then as 'lace-curtain' bourgeois, until reaching the heady heights of the Fitzgeralds moving into City Hall and the Kennedys into the White House. The Italians make up an equally lively community, based in the town's North End. The African-American community, with a proud past in Boston as the first freed slaves, is largely concentrated in Roxbury and Dorchester.

Boston is a good town to walk around. The narrow streets of the most interesting sections make driving difficult, and parking is almost impossible. Park your car outside the city and take the 'T' subway (underground) to the city's heart, **Boston Common**. Between Tremont, Boylston, and Beacon streets is the green nucleus of the 50 acres (20 hectares) that the Massachusetts Bay Company bought from a beleaguered hermit, the Reverend William Blackstone, in 1634. Already here when the 900 Puritans arrived from England, he sold out when he couldn't take any more of their officious manners. As if to make his point, they established on the green, as well as the usual grazing for livestock, a pillory and stocks, whipping post, sinners' cage, and gallows. Today the Common is popular with students and residents alike playing baseball and touch football.

Immediately west of the Common is the **Public Garden**, reclaimed in the 19th century from the marshes south of the Charles River; the neat little flower beds made up the country's first botanical garden. The artificial pond in the center provides gentle rides on board its **swan boats** in summer, and ice skating in winter. The **Visitors' Information Center** is on the Tremont Street side of the Common, a good place for maps and brochures and orientation for the 1½-mile (2.5km) **Freedom Trail** around the city's principal historical sights. The route is marked by a painted red line or by red bricks set in the sidewalk.

Tranquil-looking, white-steepled **Park Street Church** was built in 1809. At one time this was called Brimstone Corner – as the church served as a gunpowder mill during the war of 1812. The first anti-slavery speeches were delivered from its pulpit in 1829 by abolitionist William Lloyd Garrison. In the church's **Old Granary Burial Ground** are buried Paul Revere, Sam Adams, and John Hancock, signatories to the Declaration of Independence. Children may be interested in the tombstone of Mary Goose, said to be the original Mother Goose of nursery rhyme fame.

The **Old South Meeting House** (Washington and Milk streets), originally a Puritan church (1729) and now a museum of the Revolution, is best remembered as the place where Sam Adams planned the dastardly Tea Party. The British used it as a

Revere's Ride

Thanks to Henry Wadsworth Longfellow's exciting if frequently mis-leading poem, Paul Revere got all the glory for the ride to alert the fighting men of Lexington and Concord that the British were coming. In fact he was, luckily, not alone. The Royalists caught up with him soon after he reached Lexington; his co-riders William Dawes and Sam Prescott carried the news on to Concord. All the same, Revere's versatility and devotion to the American cause won him a prominent place in history.

He also rode with important Massachusetts legislative resolutions to the First Continental Congress in Philadelphia.

An accomplished silversmith, he made the noble Liberty Bowl, on show at Boston's Museum of Fine Arts. And he was one of the 'Mohawks' at the Boston Tea Party.

riding school during their occupation of Boston, burning the pews and pulpits for firewood, but the rest of the original woodwork is intact.

Farther along Washington Street, the **Old State House** (1712) was the British Governor's Residence, and it is still graced by the lion and unicorn of the royal coat of arms (copies of the originals that were burned on Independence Day, 1776). A monument marks the spot where Crispus Attucks, an African-American man and the first martyr of the Revolution, was shot.

Park Street Church

Faneuil Hall (rhymes with 'panel'), 75 State Street, has been called the 'cradle of liberty' because it is the site of two centuries of speeches by politicians from Sam Adams to John F. Kennedy. Susan B. Anthony spoke out here against the slavery both of African-Americans and of women.

From Faneuil Hall, make your way via Union and Marshall streets under the Fitzgerald Expressway to **North End**, now the center of the Italian community, with fresh pasta shops, aromatic grocery stores, and pizza parlors, amid charming old houses topped by attractive roof gardens.

Resume the Freedom Trail here on North Square at the wooden-frame **Paul Revere House** (tel: 617-523-2338; www. paulreverehouse.org), the oldest house in Boston, built soon after the disastrous city fire of 1676. The Revolutionary hero moved here in 1770, five years before he set off to make his historic ride, famously alerting New Englanders to the emergency that 'the British are coming.'

Elegant houses in Beacon Hill

The horseman's statue can be seen north of his house on Paul Revere Mall, with the fine **Old North Church** (1723) behind him. It was in the church tower, designed in the style of Christopher Wren and restored after being toppled in a 1954 hurricane, that two lanterns were hung to signal to Revere that the British were marching out. An interesting feature is the unusually tall pew boxes. These were built for parishioners to huddle in against the fierce Boston winter winds.

The Freedom Trail continues across Charlestown Bridge to the site of the Revolutionary War's first pitched battle at **Bunker Hill**, which was attended by George Washington, a general in the American Army. But if that's enough history for the time being, you can make your way back to Faneuil Hall.

To the east of it is **Faneuil Hall Marketplace**, a lively haven tucked among the administrative buildings of Government Center and the newer skyscraper office blocks. This center of boutiques, galleries, restaurants, and cafés is one of the country's most successful pieces of urban restoration.

The central domed building is Quincy Market, specializing in gourmet foods. South Market offers art galleries, jewelry, and gift stores, while North Market has fashion boutiques.

Recapture the city's old serenity on **Beacon Hill**, the handsome neighborhood sandwiched between Government Center and the Common. Here among the cedars and chestnuts and gas lanterns of **Mount Vernon Street** and Louisburg Square, you can admire the restrained glories of Boston's finest residential architecture. Boston-born Charles Bulfinch was one of the principal designers of the US Capitol in Washington, DC, as well as America's first native-born professional architect. He developed his signature Federal-style houses here in the city, and the fine but simple red-brick facades are the very essence of New England dignity.

Louisburg Square, with its residents' fenced-off garden in the center and the three-story curved, bow-fronted houses, will re-mind some of Georgian London. Others are modeled with the popular Doric-columned porches of Greek Revival.

This can be seen in its most monumental form in Bulfinch's **Massachusetts State House**, off Beacon Street, which was com-pleted in 1798, after the cornerstone was laid by Paul Revere and Sam Adams in 1785. It was this building, with its impres-sive doric portico and gilded dome, that earned Bulfinch the Washington commissions, and his place in architectural history.

Back Bay, west of the Public Garden, was a bay at the rear of Boston's 19th-century city center until landfill turned it into a residential neighborhood with a Victorian character for the city's merchants. Now it is enlivened by chic boutiques and art galleries, and is dominated by the Hancock and Prudential skyscrapers.

Both buildings offer excellent observation decks on their top floors, although the architecturally more satisfying of the two is I.M. Pei's elegant **John Hancock Tower** on Trinity Place at St James Avenue, sheathed in reflective glass. There's a grand view from the 60th floor (half a minute in the elevator) over Cambridge and Charlestown all the way to the New Hampshire mountains. Be sure to check that these observation decks are open before you set out.

Inside the Museum of Science

Museums in Boston

Museum of Fine Arts (465 Huntington Avenue; tel: 617-267-9300; www.mfa.org): One of the country's best collections. American, European, and Asian works are well laid out. Don't miss I.M. Pei's west wing.

Isabella Stewart Gardner Museum (280 The Fenway; tel: 617-566-1401; www.gardnermuseum.org): Great European collection in a building that recalls a Venetian *palazzo*.

Children's Museum (Museum Wharf, 300 Congress Street; tel: 617-426-8855; www.bostonchildrensmuseum.org): Children can blow giant bubbles, visit a Japanese house, and climb through a multilevel maze. There's an indoor play area and a 'supermarket' for smaller kids.

Museum of Science (Science Park; tel: 617-723-2500; www.mos.org): Innovative exhibits in paleontology, physiology, light and perception, a full-immersion virtual fish tank, a real fish hatchery, planetarium, IMAX theater, and the interactive Cahners ComputerPlace.

***Beaver II*, Tea Party Ship** (Congress Street Bridge on Harbor Walk, Pier 1, Pratt Street): A replica of one of the British ships raided in the protests against the duties on tea.

Cambridge (MASSACHUSETTS)

There is more to see in Cambridge (separated from Boston by the Charles River) than the prestigious college **Harvard**. Founded by the Massachusetts Bay Colony as America's first university in 1636, it is named for a young churchman, John Harvard, who bequeathed it £780, half his worldly wealth, and his library of 320 books. Now the college has an endowment of $6.2 billion and about 100 libraries with over 10 million volumes. In 1965, Harvard merged with Radcliffe College for women (founded in 1894), and the combined institutions now number over 36,000 students.

At the western end of Massachusetts Avenue, **Harvard Square** is a good introduction to the town, with cafés, restaurants, bookstores, and the 'Coop' (short for 'cooperative' but pronounced like a chicken coop), reputedly the country's biggest university store. For orientation around the campus, start at the **Information Center** in the rather daunting modern block of **Holyoke Center**, just south of the square. The campus is centered mainly around **Harvard Yard**. Unlike university architecture elsewhere in the country, Harvard avoids the 'Collegiate Gothic' of spired towers with the more traditional New England style of red brick, still seen in **Massachusetts Hall** (1720) and **Harvard Hall** (1766), along with the clapboard of **Wadsworth House** (1727), formerly the home of college presidents. The one concession to Gothic Revival is **Memorial Hall** (1878), a Victorian structure commemorating Harvard's fallen in the Civil War.

Fall in Massachusetts

The lovely 18th-century houses along Brattle Street, west of Harvard Square, are known as Tory Row after their Loyalist owners. At No. 105 is the **Longfellow National Historical Site**, poet Henry Wadsworth Longfellow's home from 1837 to 1882. Built in 1759, it was General Washington's headquarters for the siege of Boston. Most noteworthy of the campus's modern buildings is the **Carpenter Center for the Visual Arts** (24 Quincy Street; tel: 617-495-3251: www.ves.fas. harvard.edu), the only building in North America by influential architect Le Corbusier.

The **Geological and Mineralogical Museum** exhibits minerals, gems, and meteorites, and a dramatic model of a Hawaiian volcano. At the **Museum of Comparative Zoology**, look for the world's oldest egg (65 million years old) and the 25,000-year-old Harvard Mastodon, found in New Jersey in 1844. The **Botanical Museum** is also known as the Glass Flower Museum for over 3,000 plant specimens modeled life-size in glass at the Dresden workshop of Leopold and Rudolf Blaschka.

If you return to Boston via Harvard Bridge, stop off at the **Massachusetts Institute of Technology** along Massachusetts Avenue. The **MIT Museum** (tel: 617-253-5927; http://web.mit.edu) joins imagination and technology in exhibits of kinetic light sculptures, holography, artificial intelligence, and stroboscopy, while the Hart Nautical Gallery celebrates innovation in the exploration and maintenance of our oceans. The campus rewards the visitor with striking buildings designed by Finnish architect Eero Saarinen: the Kresge Auditorium and the **MIT Chapel** on Amhurst Street.

Excursions from Boston

Lexington (*MASSACHUSETTS*): *(From Boston, take Interstate 93 to the Woburn exit west)* Almost engulfed by the expanding web of metropolitan Boston, Lexington still has the classical elements of a small New England country town. There's an immaculate **village green**, with a tavern on one side and a church on the other.

This was the town into which Paul Revere rode on the evening of April 18, 1775, to warn colonial leaders John Hancock and Sam Adams that the British were coming. Their target: American arms and ammunition in nearby Concord. The tavern is Buckman Tavern, which served as rallying point for 77 Minutemen, rustic militia so called because they had to be ready at a minute's notice. At one end of the village green is a statue of the Minutemen's leader, Captain Parker. At the other, inscribed on a boulder of the **Revolutionary Monument**, are the captain's heroic words: 'Stand your ground; don't fire unless fired upon; but if they mean to have a war, let it begin here.'

It did, at 5am on April 19, when the first of 700 British soldiers arrived. The British ordered the militia to disperse, but a shot rang out and the British opened fire. In the skirmish, eight Minutemen died, and the wounded were taken to **Buckman Tavern**, which you can see today restored to

Minuteman Monument on Lexington Green

its 18th-century glory. For those who spare a thought for the poor British – they did suffer 272 casualties before they got back to Boston from this fateful sortie – there are also guided tours of the 17th-century **Munroe Tavern**, which doubled as the British field hospital and headquarters.

Salem (MASSACHUSETTS): *(North on Route 1 and 1A from Boston)* Salem is known primarily as the site of the USA's most infamous witchcraft trials; it's also famed for its more glorious maritime past.

In 1692, a slave's tales of sorcery had a strong effect on two young Puritan girls. Their gossip led to mass hysteria, witch hunts, and the hanging of 19 'witches.' For the best retelling of this gory story, visit the multimedia exhibit at the **Salem Witch Museum** (tel: 978-744-1692; www.salemwitchmuseum.com) on Washington Square. The 17th-century **Witch House** on Essex Street, home of witch-trial judge Jonathan Corwin, is restored and worth a visit.

With the witchcraft era behind it, Salem soon became a prosperous seaport and home to America's first millionaires. Down at Derby Wharf, **Salem Maritime National Historic Site** tells the story of Salem's great seafaring days; the old **Customs House** across the street can also be visited. Ship owners made a fortune out of the China trade, and many of their spoils – from Burma, India, Indonesia, China, Japan, and Korea – are now on display at the **Peabody Essex Museum** (tel: 978-744-3390; www.pem.org), the oldest continuously operating museum in America. The same museum also protects several splendid houses on Essex Street.

At No. 128 is the **Gardner-Pingree House** (1804), by Salem architect Samuel McIntire – an outstanding example of the Federal style. Note the simple elegance of the rose-brick facade topped by a white-wood balustrade and the wonderful woodwork of the

Cape Cod is famed for its beautiful beaches

interior. The Peirce-Nichols House (1782) at 80 Federal Street is also by McIntire.

Salem is also known as the birthplace and home of 19th-century novelist Nathaniel Hawthorne, who worked at the Customs House. His **House of the Seven Gables** (54 Turner Street; tel: 978-744-0991; www.7gables.org) on the waterfront, is the oldest living history museum in the US.

Besides being a historic treasure, Salem, with its green common, traffic-free center, and restored waterfront (visit the stores and restaurants on pretty **Pickering Wharf**) is a lovely place to wander.

Cape Cod (MASSACHUSETTS): *(Interstate 93 out of Boston, Route 3 to the Cape)* The beaches, sand dunes, and marshlands of Cape Cod's east coast are both invigorating and relaxing. It was a surprise to no one when, in 1961, President Kennedy made the coast a protected area – the **Cape Cod National Seashore**. It had, after all, been his family's holiday home for years.

The easiest way to reach the National Seashore is via the high-speed ferry to **Provincetown**, at the northern tip of Cape Cod. Provincetown itself is a busy tourist center with plenty of boutiques and galleries, renowned for its 'anything goes' attitude (it's one of the the the East Coast's main gay meccas).

But here on the outer elbow facing the Atlantic Ocean you can listen to the pounding surf and stroll the awesome beaches that are backed by huge dunes. Access to the dunes is strictly controlled and limited to boardwalks at some points. The National Seashore has two information centers: the Salt Pond Visitor Center, near Eastham on Route 6, and the smaller Province Lands Visitor Center just outside Provincetown. At Province Lands, take the opportunity to climb onto the roof for a panoramic view of the dunes. Another great view can be had from a hillock northwest of Pilgrim Lake in the **Pilgrim Heights** area. The **Pilgrim Spring Trail** takes you to a spot where, according to local legend, in 1620 the people of the *Mayflower* drank their first American fresh water.

At the southernmost tip of Cape Cod, Woods Hole ferries go across to Martha's Vineyard (45-minute crossing) and Nantucket (three hours) – two island resorts that are popular with discerning New Englanders and New Yorkers.

There are no wild grapes growing on **Martha's Vineyard** anymore, but the local population drinks plenty of wine. You can get around the island by shuttle bus or rent a bicycle or moped. The beaches are excellent, Katama on the south shore being favored by surfers. For a lovely view, go west of Katama up onto the **Gay Head Cliffs**, which consist of layers of colored clay – red, orange, gray, blue, and ocher. The local Indians turn this clay into pottery. Equally brightly colored are the charming gingerbread cottages of **Oak Bluffs**, while the grander houses of **Edgartown** are made of sparkling white clapboard.

Nantucket Island is a good family resort. The beaches on the north side of the island are washed by the warm waters of the Gulf Stream, and offer easy swimming. Hardier swimmers go to Cisco and Surfside for the big breakers of the south shore.

Nantucket town, beautifully preserved on the cobbled **Main Street**, had a proud whaling history that ended abruptly in the second half of the 19th century when Pennsylvania oil replaced whale blubber; at the **Whaling Museum** (Broad Street) is all the sailor's paraphernalia of the whaling industry. If you're taken by the impressive exhibition of scrimshaw, you may want to buy some in the waterfront stores on **Straight Wharf**, at the end of Main Street.

Plymouth (MASSACHUSETTS): On your way from Boston to Cape Cod, stop off on Route 3 to pay homage to the site of New England's founding. A boulder on the edge of the harbor is said to be the legendary **Plymouth Rock** onto which the first Pilgrim from the *Mayflower* stepped in 1620. Today, the boulder is protected by monumental granite pillars. North of the rock, at State Pier, is *Mayflower II*, a replica that sailed from England in 1957. Just south of the town is **Plimoth Plantation** (tel: 508-746-1622; www.plimoth.org; closed winter months), a living museum of the Pilgrims' first village of 1627: thatch-roofed, clapboard cottages with period English furniture, barns, and stables. Costumed actors playing historical individuals charm with their 17th-century world view and dialect. Nearby is a replica of a period Wampanoag encampment.

The Berkshires (*MASSACHUSETTS*): (*Interstate 90 from Boston or Interstate 87 from New York*) The rolling foothills at the western end of Massachusetts at the border with New York state, loosely called the Berkshires, offer wonderful opportunities in the summer to combine music, dance, and

Plimouth Plantation

theater with hiking and fishing. The Berkshires are the place for watching the fall foliage, and there's skiing in winter. Dotted among the hills are the grand 19th-century estates that provided summer homes for wealthy New Yorkers and Bostonians and are now resort hotels.

Since 1934, the **Tanglewood** estate (just outside Lenox) has been home to the summer Berkshire Music Festival. Its Music Shed, designed by Finnish architect Eero Saarinen, seats 6,000 people. A nice way to enjoy the concerts is to come for a picnic a couple of hours early and listen to the music (at a much lower price) from the lawn. The Chamber Music Hall holds other concerts.

The Berkshire Theater Festival is at the Playhouse in **Stockbridge** (south of Tanglewood on Route 7). The town itself is well worth a visit. It was established in 1734 by four families who had the goal of converting the local Mohican tribe to Christianity. Reverend John Sergeant's **Mission House** (1739), Route 102, austere and even gloomy by modern standards but considered plush in its day, is now a museum of that pious era.

The **Old Corner House**, appropriately on Main Street, was the home of painter/illustrator Norman Rockwell, respected observer of American Main Street life for the covers of the *Saturday Evening Post* magazine. The **Norman Rockwell Museum** (Route 183; tel: 413-298-4100; www.nrm.org) documents the evolution of his work, from the details of small-town Americana in the Depression years to the more recent struggles of racial integration and urban violence, and covers other well-known illustrators (Rockwell Kent, Maxfield Parrish) as well.

Farther south, around **Great Barrington**, there is first-class fishing and hiking along the Housatonic Valley.

MID-ATLANTIC REGION

Seven years after the end of the War of Independence, the northern and southern states finally agreed on a site for the nation's permanent capital – right between the two regions, on land ceded by the states of Maryland and Virginia. A visit to Washington, DC and a journey through the surrounding states will let you compare the businesslike North with the more leisurely South.

▶ Washington, DC (DISTRICT OF COLUMBIA)

Washington, DC's architecture leans more to the temples of ancient Greece and Rome than to the palaces and cathedrals of European monarchies, and the government buildings are in a green and pleasant setting. The 69 sq. miles (179 sq. km) of the District of Columbia include 33 parks, relics of the old Maryland estates and plantations.

Over 3 million people live in Greater Metropolitan Washington and the suburbs in Virginia and Maryland; the city itself numbers just under 600,000 residents (582,000 in a

2006 census, down from 606,900 in 1990), more than half of them African-American.

When you see the attractive houses and diplomatic missions around Massachusetts Avenue, and the university district of Georgetown, you may find it hard to believe that for a long time Washington was just marshland on the banks of the Potomac River. To lay out the new capital, George Washington called on the Paris-born engineer Pierre-Charles L'Enfant, the man who remodeled Federal Hall in New York for the presidential inauguration.

But the Frenchman, a major with the US Army during the Revolutionary War, produced a radical plan for the central federal district inspired by Rome and Versailles, which proved a little too ambitious for the young Republic's Treasury. After a quarrel with the bureaucracy, who called him 'L'Enfant terrible,' he was fired and died in misery, although his designs for the city were later more fully realized.

The Capitol and North Fountain, Washington, DC

Apart from the White House – only half finished when John Adams took up residence in 1800 – the place looked much like a ramshackle frontier town for most of the 19th century, in part because it was sacked and burned by the British in 1814. The Capitol took 70 years to complete, and the streets weren't paved or properly lit until after the Civil War. It was only in the 20th century that Washington assumed the shape of L'Enfant's grand conception – perhaps it took that long to find the money – and the architect was reburied, with honors, at Arlington National Cemetery.

Considering all there is to be seen, the area covering Washington's sights is surprisingly compact. It's practically all in a rectangle extending from Union Station and the Library of Congress, in the east, to Watergate and the Lincoln Memorial near the Potomac River, in the west. Georgetown is just northwest of this rectangle, and Arlington National Cemetery is on the west bank of the Potomac. Nearly all the monuments and museums are free of charge.

When you don't feel like walking – Washington can be very hot and sticky in high summer – an agreeable alternative is the system of open-sided Tourmobile shuttle trolleys. These follow a route past the city's main monuments, museums, and government buildings, stopping at convenient points around the Capitol, the Mall, and the White House. Guides provide cheerful commentaries as you ride. The advantage is that you can get on and off

The White House

as often as you like with one all-day ticket (bought on the trolley when you first board). The Tourmobile also undertakes excursions to Arlington and Mount Vernon *(see pages 94 and 99)*.

Public transportation in Washington includes an efficient municipal bus service together with an extensive underground Metrorail network. Taxis are plentiful, charging – not exorbitantly – by the zones into which the town is divided (see the map in the cab) rather than by the meter. Zone One covers most of the main sights. Keep your car for out-of-town excursions, because legal parking Downtown is expensive, and illegal parking is disastrous. The police do not hesitate to tow vehicles away to one of 20 compounds without letting you know which one.

The White House *(1600 Pennsylvania Avenue, NW*; tel: 202-456-7041; www.whitehouse.gov*)*: Although the White House used to be open to the public, because of anti-terrorism precautions, there are now only limited tours; these are generally available only to American citizens who can arrange them through their congressional representative. But you can still get a reasonable sense of the White House and its history if you stop by the **Visitor Center** at 15th and E streets in the Department of Commerce building. Park Rangers who staff the center are helpful and there are several exhibits, a 30-minute film, and a gift shop. There are occasional tours of the White House gardens for the general public, with tickets distributed at 8am on the day of each tour. Contact the Visitor Center for more information.

The White House was designed in 1792 by Irish-born architect James Hoban in the English Palladian style popular with the landed gentry. In the competition for a $500 gold medal, Hoban beat an anonymous entry by Thomas Jefferson.

Happy to reside there himself in 1801, Jefferson declared the building 'big enough for two emperors, one Pope and the grand Lama.' That opinion didn't discourage him from promptly adding a terrace pavilion on either side while Benjamin Latrobe was putting on the porticoes. This set the pattern for nearly all Jefferson's successors – though without the benefit of his architectural training – of remodeling or redecorating their temporary home.

Visitors lucky enough to go inside the White House follow roughly the following tour: on the ground floor is a corridor that looks out onto the Jacqueline Kennedy Garden, then the Vermeil Room (with its collection of gilded silver serving pieces) and the Library. Upstairs is the State Floor, containing the five rooms that are most familiar to the public from books and TV.

The **East Room**, where presidential press conferences are held, is used for concerts, balls, and receptions – weddings for the president's children, funeral services for presidents who die in office, notably Lincoln, Franklin D. Roosevelt, and Kennedy. The White House's first First Lady, Abigail Adams, used it as a drying room for her laundry. The famous 1796 Gilbert Stuart portrait of George Washington was saved from the 1814 fire by Dolley Madison, wife of President James Madison.

First ladies often hold tea parties in the elegant **Green Room** under a wonderful 1790 cut-glass chandelier given by the British government to President Herbert Hoover. Jefferson liked to take his dinner in the Green Room, showing off to baffled Americans the latest gourmet ideas he'd imported from Europe, such as macaroni, waffles, and ice cream.

Toasting the White House

It wasn't always the president who 'redesigned' the White House. In 1814, the dastardly British Admiral George Cockburn led an assault on Washington and the White House in retaliation for American pillage in Canada. While President James Madison had gone off to join the militia, wife Dolley stayed behind to take care of the valuables, getting out just before the British arrived and set fire to the place. A providential thunderstorm put out the fire, but not before the White House turned decidedly black.

The **Blue Room** is decorated in French Empire style appropriate to the state dinners held here. Outside the windows is 'Truman's Balcony', where the president from Missouri used to take the air. The **Red Room** with its red-satin walls has impressive gilded and marble tables. Its opulence contrasts with the restrained decor of the **State Dining Room** at the western end of this floor (which is underneath the presidential living quarters). Dominated by a portrait of Abraham Lincoln,

Washington Monument

it's done in fine 18th-century English style, walnut Queen Anne chairs against oak paneling with Corinthian pilasters.

The Mall and Potomac Park: The Mall – an expanse of greenery and water stretching from the Capitol to the Lincoln Memorial, crossing the axis between the White House and the Tidal Basin at the Washington Monument – is one of the country's great urban vistas. It is almost always full of people strolling, lounging, flying kites, and playing ball, surrounded by monuments and museums. It's a posthumous triumph for planner Pierre-Charles L'Enfant, whose dream it had been to achieve this harmonious interplay of the built environment with nature.

If the Statue of Liberty represents America to the world, then the **Washington Monument** symbolizes the nation to Americans. Construction of the 555ft (169m) white marble obelisk began in 1848 but dragged on for 36 years because of lack of funds and the interruption of the Civil War. There's an elevator to the top, with its great views of the city.

Abraham Lincoln, immortalized in the Lincoln Memorial

West of the obelisk, wander along the tree-lined, 2,000ft (610m) long reflecting pool to the **Lincoln Memorial** (1922). This Greek-temple-like structure, a white rectangular box surrounded by 36 Doric columns, houses the 19ft (6m) seated statue of a pensive Abraham Lincoln created by Daniel Chester French. There is a wonderful effect at daybreak when the sculpture is first lit by the rising sun.

On the left of the entrance is a plaque with Lincoln's speech after the Battle of Gettysburg during the Civil War, when he paid tribute to those who had died for a 'nation conceived in liberty and dedicated to the proposition that all men are created equal.' American schoolchildren know this speech as the Gettysburg Address.

Pause at the **Vietnam Veterans Memorial** nearby. This simple monument to the Vietnam war dead carries the names of 58,000 soldiers. The more conventional statuary group was added later at the request of many of those who served. From here you can make a detour across Potomac Park and around the Tidal Basin to the **Jefferson Memorial** (1943), inspired by the Pantheon in Rome.

As you look at the bronze statue of this architect, philosopher, and most elegant of statesmen, you might recall the eloquent words of President Kennedy. At a dinner given in the Blue Room of the White House for Nobel Prize winners, he said, 'I think this is the most extraordinary collection of talent, of human knowledge, that has ever been gathered together at the White House – with the possible exception of when Thomas Jefferson dined alone.'

The Mall leads past one of the world's most impressive concentrations of museums and galleries *(see pages 97–9)*. South of the brooding statue of Civil War General Ulysses S. Grant, stop off at the **Botanic Garden**. A three-year renovation added new environmental exhibits to this extensive and fragrant international collection.

Capitol Hill: The most powerful government in the Western world deserves a setting like the **Capitol**. This massive edifice imposes its will under a huge white dome that joins the Senate in the north wing to the House of Representatives in the south; the place exudes power.

William Thornton's original design in 1793 was a low-domed affair. When Benjamin Latrobe expanded the design after the British burning of 1814, the homespun Congressmen complimented him only on the corncobs and tobacco leaves with which he rather whimsically decorated the Corinthian columns of their chamber. Charles Bulfinch came from Boston to put on a bigger and better dome, but in 1850 Congress decided it should be even bigger. So Thomas Walter, with nothing less than St Peter's in Rome for his model, hoisted an iron dome up on a grandiose columned 'drum' and that, with Thomas Crawford's statue *Freedom* topping it off in 1863, is the way it stands today.

The Capitol is entered from the east side, starting at the **Rotunda** (there are normally 45-minute guided tours). The vast ceiling is decorated by a fresco painted by Constantino Brumidi in 1865, *The Apotheosis of George Washington*, showing him glorified by the deities of Liberty, Victory, and Fame and 13 ladies representing the 13 original states. Below is a 300ft (91m) frieze devoted to American historical events, from Columbus through Cornwallis's surrender of the British Army at Yorktown to the flight of the Wright brothers' aircraft in 1903.

In **Statuary Hall** and the corridors leading off the Rotunda, you'll see what is widely regarded as one of the most delightfully horrendous sculpture collections in America. It's the result of an act of cultural democracy by which each of the 50 states was invited to exhibit its most famous citizens, portrayed by the state's own sculptors.

Outside, the Capitol's grounds cover 131 acres (53 hectares) of charming parkland designed by the 19th-century landscape architect Frederick Law Olmsted, well known for his parks in New York, Boston, Chicago, and California.

The **Library of Congress** (1st Street and Independence Avenue; tel: 202-707-9779; www.loc.gov), packed with millions of books, maps, manuscripts, periodicals, photographs, recordings, and rare instruments, is one of the great institutions of Capitol Hill. For visitors, the permanent exhibition of documents includes a 1455 Gutenberg Bible, one of only three in the world to have survived in perfect condition. Also look at the poignant Civil War photographs of Matthew Brady, first of the great American photojournalists, in the Prints and Photographs section.

Behind the Library of Congress, the **Folger Library** (201 East Capitol Street) offers in its Tudor interior the largest collection of Shakespeareana outside Britain, including a nicely reproduced Elizabethan theater. Next door, the awe-inspiring **Supreme Court**, built in 1935, is the last of Washington's government buildings in the Graeco-Roman style.

Library of Congress

The library has 138 million items, including books and rare photographs. There is a permanent staff of 3,700.

North and South of the Mall: The scene of Abraham Lincoln's assassination, **Ford's Theatre** (511 10th Street, between E and F streets; tel: 202-

The Supreme Court, built in 1935

347-4833; www.fordstheatre.org), is a National Historic Site, meticulously restored to how it looked on the fateful evening of April 14, 1865. Since 1968, it has been operating again as a theater, complete with presidential box. The basement is now a museum of Lincoln's life. It preserves the clothes he wore to the play, the Derringer pistol that killed him, and the diary of assassin John Wilkes Booth, Shakespearean actor and embittered supporter of the lost Southern cause. Across the street, at No. 516, is **Petersen House**, where the dying president was taken – the streets too badly paved for a safe trip back to the White House. You'll see the bleak little bedroom where the 6ft 4-inch (2m) Lincoln had to be laid diagonally across the bed.

For a lesson in history, visit the **National Archives** (Constitution Avenue between 7th and 9th streets; www.archives.gov), where you can see the original documents of the Declaration of Independence, the Constitution, and the Bill of Rights, all handwritten on parchment. Some have faded badly but are now surrounded by light-filtering glass, with helium protection against decay.

South of the Mall, at 14th and C streets, is the **Bureau of Engraving and Printing** (tel: 877-874-4114; www.bep.treas. gov; valid photo ID required; tours cancelled during times of heightened security), where you can see the printing of US paper money and postage stamps, from a one-cent stamp to a $500 million Treasury Note (no photographs allowed). Follow the journey of the blank white sheets made of cotton and linen through inking and cutting to the stacking of crisp dollar bills at the other end. You can buy shredded money for a souvenir.

Arlington (Virginia): Running north behind the Lincoln Parkway between Rock Creek Parkway and the river is a delightful half-mile walk along the green riverbank. On weekends you can see polo, field hockey, and canoes paddling by. You'll pass the **Kennedy Center for the Performing Arts** (2700 F Street), less admired for its clumsy architecture than for its cultural activities in a capital that previously neglected the performing arts. The cen-

Arlington National Cemetery

ter comprises two theaters, an opera house, a concert hall, and the American Film Institute's excellent 'cinémathèque.' Farther north is **Watergate**, a complex of apartments where in 1972 dirty tricks were perpetrated, resulting in the downfall of President Richard Nixon, who was forced to resign rather than face impeachment.

Beautifully situated on a hillside on the opposite bank of the Potomac is **Arlington House** (also known as the the the Robert E. Lee Memorial; www.nps.gov/arho). This sober Greek Revival mansion fronted by eight Doric columns was built by George Washington's adopted grandson, George Washington P. Custis, in 1812. It was later the home of General Robert E. Lee until he left to lead the Confederate armies in 1861. Immediately in front of the house is the grave of the architect Pierre-Charles L'Enfant, commanding the best view across the river of the capital he so lovingly planned. A granite slab is engraved with his original plan. It's a chance to compare the plan with the result. Arlington House is undergoing restoration until 2010. It remains open, but all furnishings have been removed until completion.

During the Civil War, Union troops confiscated Lee's house, and part of its surrounding plantation was used as a burial ground for the war dead. Out of this grew **Arlington National Cemetery**, in which only American soldiers who have seen active duty can be buried.

Pride of place goes to the **Tomb of the Unknowns** (soldiers of the two World Wars and the Korean War), guarded by a solitary infantryman ceremoniously changed every half-hour in summer, every hour in winter. In its own small park, the **John F. Kennedy Grave** is a square of simple paving set around an eternal flame. Jacqueline Kennedy Onassis is buried in the same plot, and John's brother Robert Kennedy is buried nearby.

The Marine Corps War Memorial, better known as the **Iwo Jima Statue**, is located outside the north entrance to the cemetery. Standing 78ft (23m) high, this is the world's tallest bronze statue, featuring five marines and a sailor hoisting the American flag (a real one is raised daily by Washington-based marines) on

Mt Suribachi during the battle for the Japanese Pacific island base of Iwo Jima on February 23, 1945. It took three more weeks to capture the island, with the loss of over 5,000 men – but Japanese losses were four times higher.

▶ **Georgetown:** Northwest of the Downtown federal district, Georgetown is the home of Washington's elite in government, the diplomatic corps, university establishments, and better-paid journalists. It's also a lively part of town, with bright, pleasant stores, art galleries, cafés, and restaurants, centered on M Street and Wisconsin Avenue.

Georgetown was laid out in 1751 and was already established as a major tobacco market when the town of Washington was still being planned. Georgetown exported tobacco along the Potomac and imported luxury goods such as silks, wines, tinware, tea, and powder for the wigs of its high-stepping gentry. A couple of houses survive from that era, but most of its better residential architecture is Georgian and Federal in style from the first half of the 19th century, with a few Victorians from after the Civil War. Its narrow, shaded streets are a fine change from the broad avenues of governmental Washington.

The oldest house in town is the 1766 **Old Stone House**, at 3051 M Street, now a museum of colonial life. Another noteworthy Georgian edifice is **Dumbarton House** (2715 Q Street), remodeled by Benjamin Latrobe in 1805. It's now a museum of federal period furniture, silver, and china. Its public programs include lectures on 18th- and 19th-century furniture styles as well as concerts.

Dumbarton Oaks (3101 R Street), an imposing mansion built in 1801, was the site of the 1944 conference at which the US, Britain, the Soviet Union, and China drew up the blueprint for the United Nations. The 16 acres (6.5 hectares) of grounds are a delightful mixture of formal terraces and pools with more informal English-style landscaping on a lower level. The gardens include (at the 32nd Street entrance) the mushroom-domed Museum of Pre-Columbian and Byzantine Art, designed by Philip Johnson.

At the southern edge of Georgetown is the remnant of the **Chesapeake & Ohio Canal** (the 'C&O'). Serving as an artery for coal-hauling from 1828 to 1924, it now welcomes walkers, cyclists, canoeists, and fishermen – and in winter, skaters. **Canal Square** (1054 31st Street) is an old canalside warehouse converted into a shopping center.

Museums in Washington

National Gallery of Art (Constitution Avenue between 4th and 6th streets; tel: 202-737-4215; www.nga.gov): The West Building, a classical, columned temple of art, is devoted to European and American paint-

Enjoy the ride in Georgetown

ing and sculpture, with exhibits from the Middle Ages to the present day. I.M. Pei's design of the East Building is a breathtaking combination of geometric forms – soaring triangles segmented into piercing angles. The effect is even more exhilarating inside, where the museum's collection of contemporary art is on display.

Smithsonian Institution: Not one museum but a huge umbrella collection grouping many – 17 museums in Washington, two in New York and affiliates in other cities. The museums have a combined inventory of 75 million artistic and scientific items, only 1 percent of which are ever on display. All are free. The distinctive red sandstone building on the Mall, commonly called 'the Castle,' is the Smithsonian Visitors' Center, open daily, which also has a café. The following nine museums are all part of the Smithsonian; for information on any of them, telephone 202-633-1000.

National Air and Space Museum (7th Street and Independence Avenue; www.nasm.si.edu): The entire history of flying, from the Wright brothers' first lift across a meadow in North Carolina in 1903 to Neil Armstrong's journey just 66 years later from Cape Canaveral to the moon and back, is packed into these 23 galleries.

National Museum of Natural History (10th Street and Constitution Avenue; www.mnh.si.edu): Everything from an 80ft (24m) long diplodocus to the creepy, crawly Insect Zoo. The Sant Ocean Hall is the largest permanent exhibition.

National Museum of American History (Madison Drive, 12th to 14th streets; www.americanhistory.si.edu): Depicts US life from different periods and social strata, with definitive exhibits on the history of electric lights and motors. A major renovation, completed in late 2008, added spacious new galleries.

National Museum of the American Indian (4th Street and Independence Avenue; www.nmai.si.edu): A collection showcasing thousands of masterworks, including carvings and masks

The National Air and Space Museum

from the Northwest; quilled hides and feather bonnets from the Plains; pottery from the Southwest; 18th-century materials from the Great Lakes; and beautiful Navajo weavings.

Hirshhorn Museum (Independence Avenue between 7th and 9th streets; www.hirshhorn.si.edu): Modern art is displayed in this drum-shaped building, highlighted by a sculpture garden featuring Rodin's *Burghers of Calais* and pieces by Moore, Picasso, and David Smith. The painting collection includes examples of Cubism, Social Realism, Op, Pop, and Minimalism.

Freer Gallery of Art (Jefferson at 12th Street; www.asia.si.edu): A major Asian collection and a smaller American one. An underground exhibition space connects the Freer to the **Arthur M. Sackler Gallery** (1050 Independence Avenue SW), which has Buddhist sculpture, ancient Iranian metalwork, and works of art from China, Southeast Asia, and the ancient Near East.

National Portrait Gallery (8th and F streets; www.npg.si.edu): All the presidents and great ladies are here, including Pocahontas, Eleanor Roosevelt, and Gertrude Stein. The gallery is also a major center of historical photography.

Smithsonian American Art Musuem (8th and G streets; www.americanart.si.edu): Fine examples from colonial times via Winslow Homer, Cassatt, and Whistler to O'Keeffe and de Kooning. Its sister premises are the **Renwick Gallery** (Pennsylvania Avenue and 17th Street), where the best of American design, crafts, and decorative arts are displayed.

Excursions from Washington, DC

Mount Vernon (VIRGINIA): *(16 miles/26km south on Mt Vernon Memorial Parkway; also by Tourmobile in summer;* tel: 703-780-2000; www.mountvernon.org) More than just a dutiful pilgrimage to the home of George Washington, Mount Vernon offers a journey back to an 18th-century Virginia plantation, beautifully restored, the lawns perhaps a shade more tailored than in the old days. Make the 35-minute drive early in the morning to avoid the spring and summer crowds and sit, as George and his wife Martha did, on the square-columned veranda that overlooks the Potomac River Valley and the green Maryland hills in the distance.

A great soldier and leader of men, George Washington was also an accomplished farmer, one of the first to develop and apply extended crop-rotation plans. He owned 8,000 acres (3,250 hectares) of land, divided into five farms, and had 120 slaves to work them. At the border of Bowling Green, you'll pass old trees planted by George himself. Inside the house, you can see Martha's account books. George's bedroom has original pieces, including the portmanteau trunk that accompanied him throughout the Revolutionary War, and the bed in which he died in 1799.

> **Colonial Virginia** (*South from Washington on Interstate 95 via Richmond to State Highway 5*): Highway 5 takes you to the historic triangle of Jamestown, where Virginia was founded; Williamsburg, Virginia's capital from 1699 to 1780; and Yorktown, where the Revolutionary War reached its climax in 1781. The towns are linked by the Colonial Parkway on which a Visitors' Center dispenses tickets for Colonial Williamsburg (exit 238 off Interstate 64). If time is tight, visit all three in one day.

Colonial Williamsburg is the largest-scale restoration project in the country, with over 500 18th-century buildings. Visitors are invited to engage with its denizens (over 800 actors in period dress). Visit the cobbler's, gunsmith's, apothecary, and printer's workshops and learn about these crafts from the artisans, or take a horse-drawn carriage ride.

The restoration was carried out with funds from John D. Rockefeller, Jr, in 1927. Drawing on 18th-century engravings found in Oxford, England's Bodleian Library, architectural historians restored the 1705 **Capitol** building and **Governor's Palace** in precise detail. For the latter, they were aided by a plan of the interior drawn by Thomas Jefferson, who lived here for six months as Governor of Virginia. The major thoroughfare is **Duke of Gloucester Street**, with some of the finest wooden weatherboard and red-brick Georgian houses.

Influential Revolutionary figures met at the Raleigh Tavern; you can taste 18th-century dishes at the King's Arms, Chowning's, and Christiana Campbell's taverns, all in fine restored state.

Jamestown, 6 miles (10km) south of Williamsburg, was the site settled by the first pioneers from England in May 1607 (13 years before the *Mayflower* reached Massachusetts). For centuries it was thought that the only original relic of colonial Jamestown was a crumbling church tower, as the site was abandoned because of malarial mosquitoes (now gone). But since 1994, extensive and on-going excavations have re-

Colonial Williamsburg

vealed thousands of artifacts, including portions of the original James Fort. **Jamestown Settlement** has been built as a replica of the old palisade fort, with a lodge for glassblowing and, on the river, full-scale replicas of the tiny vessels *Susan Constant, Discovery,* and *Godspeed*, which brought John Smith and 103 settlers across the Atlantic Ocean on their long, courageous voyage.

Yorktown, 18 miles (29km) to the east, is where Lord Cornwallis surrendered his troops in October 1781, sealing Britain's loss of its American colonies. Before visiting the battlefield, stop at the **Yorktown Victory Center**, 2 miles (3km) out of town, where you can visit a 'Continental Army encampment,' talk to costumed interpreters, and see a display of Revolutionary War artifacts. In town, visit **Moore House**, where the British negotiated their capitulation with the Americans and the French.

Major Cities near Washington, DC

Baltimore and Philadelphia are interesting counterparts to Washington, DC. Baltimore, a major seaport for Chesapeake Bay, has undergone an exciting urban renewal, and is a great place for seafood, while Philadelphia is the birthplace of American nationhood and has a colorful mixture of ethnic groups.

Baltimore (*MARYLAND*): Baltimore suffers from what Baltimoreans consider unfair barbs. Poet Edgar Allan Poe died here and was buried in Westminster Churchyard, but otherwise the town is somewhat lacking in historical monuments. But it makes up for this with some of the boldest urban renewal in the country. The **Charles Center** has turned the erstwhile blight of the Downtown business district into a lively area of stores, theaters, and cafés. Equally successful and more attractive is the 95-acre (38-hectare) **Inner Harbor** development, which has transformed the once seedy waterfront of Baltimore Harbor into a stylish setting for hotels, theaters, restaurants, parks, and promenades. Art shows, concerts, and sports activities keep the place hopping throughout the year. The restaurants around the harbor serve fine seafood straight from the bay – clams and oysters, soft-shell crab, crab cakes, and a Baltimore specialty, hard-shell crabs.

At Constellation Dock you can tour the restored Navy

The Declaration of Independence was signed in Philadelphia

frigate *Constellation*, which was launched here in 1797. Landlubbers who prefer old locomotives can see a fine collection at the **Baltimore & Ohio Railroad Museum** (Poppleton and Pratt streets).

Pride of the **Baltimore Museum of Art** (Charles and 31st streets; tel: 410-396-7100; www.artbma.org) is the excellent Cone Collection of 19th- and 20th-century paintings, well endowed with works by Matisse and Picasso.

Philadelphia (*PENNSYLVANIA*): One of the more charming aspects of America is that this Pennsylvanian town that occupies such an important place in the history of the USA should also be a national joke. Philadelphia, after all, is the City of Brotherly Love that William Penn established as a model of religious freedom and colonial enterprise and where Benjamin Franklin and Thomas Jefferson championed the movement for independence. But it's also a quiet, sedate town, which comedian W.C. Fields unfavorably commemorated on his tombstone: 'better than playing Philadelphia,' and where the master of horror, Edgar Allan Poe, wrote his famous poem *The Raven*.

While the modern city has been enlivened by its Italian and Jewish communities, it's the old Anglo-Saxon backbone that sets a dignified tone. According to Mark Twain, 'In Boston, they ask "How much does he know?" In New York, "How much is he worth?" In Philadelphia, it's "Who were his parents?"'

Independence National Historical Park at the heart of old Philadelphia contains all the great buildings of early America's government, and is called the 'most historic square mile in America.' At the grand red-brick Georgian **Independence Hall** (5th and Chestnut) you can see where America's founding fathers signed the Declaration of Independence and, later, the United States Constitution. Next door, the states' representatives met in **Congress Hall** and signed the Bill of Rights that forced the government to protect rather than interfere with individual freedoms. In the **Liberty Bell Center** on Market Street between 5th and 6th streets is the famous **Liberty Bell** in its glass pavilion.

This was the bell that came from England in 1752, cracked when it was first struck in Philadelphia, was repaired in time to ring out from the tower of Independence Hall on July 4, 1776, and cracked again in the 19th century. It has not been rung since.

Take a look at magnificent **City Hall** (Market and Broad streets). The Louvre in Paris was its architectural model and, locals like to point out, it's bigger than Washington's Capitol building. On top is a statue of William Penn.

The **Philadelphia Museum of Art** (26th and the Parkway; tel: 215-763-8100; www.philamuseum.org) is very large, housing a good collection of American works, plus some fine Impressionist (Van Gogh's *Sunflowers*) and post-Impressionist paintings. It also has excellent special exhibitions. **Edgar Allan Poe's House** (532 North 7th Street) is now a museum of Poe memorabilia. He lived here with his young wife. The **Rodin Museum** (22nd and Parkway) has the biggest collection of the French sculptor's work outside Paris. The **Franklin Institute** (20th and the Parkway; tel: 215-448-1200; www2.fi.edu) is a marvelous science museum, with halls devoted to astronomy, computers, electronics, railroads, aviation, geology, weather, biology, and Franklin's experiments with electricity. There's also an IMAX theater.

The Liberty Bell

Philadelphia's original Liberty Bell was cast in England by the Whitechapel Foundry in London and delivered in 1752. It famously cracked the first time it was struck.

The same foundry was commissioned to provide an exact replacement for the bicentennial celebrations in 1976, and it now hangs in the Liberty Bell Center, bearing the inscription:

'FOR THE PEOPLE OF THE UNITED STATES OF AMERICA
FROM THE PEOPLE OF BRITAIN
4 JULY 1976
LET FREEDOM RING'

THE SOUTH

For people on vacation, the South is where the sun always shines. For an introduction, start with Florida for the exquisite hedonism of its subtropical sun, then to Charleston, South Carolina, for an echo of the golden past, over to Atlanta for a look at the 'New South,' and then to New Orleans, a grand old river city with a unique Creole flavor.

Sunset over Florida's Gulf Coast

In southern Florida's subtropical climate, with air and seawater temperatures ranging from an average low of 74°F (23°C) in January to an average high of 88°F (31°C) in August, lovers of heat should watch out. Sunbathing here should begin with no more than 30 minutes the first day; the Florida sun can scorch even when the sky is overcast.

Miami and the Beaches *(FLORIDA)*

Miami Beach: Connected to mainland Miami by causeways across Biscayne Bay, this is where the pleasure begins: 7 miles (11km) of sandy beaches in front of high-rise hotels and condominium apartments. If your hotel has commandeered its own piece of the shoreline – as is the case around 46th Street – you may be perfectly happy to stay there, but if not, there are several alternatives.

A few years ago these fine beaches nearly disappeared because of the erosion caused by undisciplined construction along the seafront. At the end of the 1970s, the US Army Corps of Engineers came to the rescue by dumping 13½ million cubic yards (10 million cubic meters) of sand along the reclaimed 100yd (91m) wide strip of seashore.

Haulover Beach, at the north end, is for the very active, with palm trees to shade lazy companions. It's well known for surfing, frisbee-tossing, and fishing off the pier. There are also barbecue grills where you can turn your catch into a picnic.

Surfside at 93rd Street and the **64th and 53rd Street beaches** are best for swimming, away from the high-end crowds that parade along Miami Beach. **21st Street** is a favorite with young people, who turn the fast-food stands into lively open-air clubs.

South Beach: An entire square mile (2.5 sq. km) of this ice-cream-cake confection known as the **Art Deco District** was listed in the National Registry of Historic Places, and there are few neighborhoods anywhere more likely to put a smile on your face. Around **Washington Avenue**, on the blocks between 8th and 21st streets, you can stroll around hotels, apartment buildings, restaurants, and stores that sprang up in the tourist boom of the 1920s and 1930s, with a flourish of chrome and bakelite, gaily colored ceramic tiles and mirrored glass, borrowing motifs from the Egyptians and Aztecs. After years of scorn by purists who found the buildings too 'florid,' South Beach and the Deco District is now not only the trendiest place in Florida, but one of the major entertainment and fashion capitals in America. Dress to kill when you come here, and try a pink cocktail. Today, everyone's a film star.

Collins Avenue stretches for many blocks of more recent hotels (i.e. 1950s), the flagship being The **Fontainebleau** at 44th Street. This 1950s style has created another architectural preservation movement in the city called 'MiMo,' which is an abbreviation of 'Miami Modern.' The Fontainebleau reopened in late 2008 after a $1 billion refit, including the building of four new towers. Even if you're not staying here, plan to have a drink and look around at this unquestionable monument to American leisure.

For a taste of ultra-modern chic of the South Beach variety, pay a visit to the **Delano Hotel** (1685 Collins Avenue). International hotelier Ian Schrager and designer Philippe Starck partnered to remodel this 1947 hotel with super-elegant austerity. The building itself is also distinctive, with its modernist finned tower.

Miami's fashionable South Beach

Metro Miami *(FLORIDA)*: Downtown is a busy area of department stores, restaurants, and nightclubs around Flagler Street and Biscayne Boulevard. But it's even livelier south of Downtown in the Cuban neighborhood of **Little Havana**, centered on a 30-block section around 'Calle Ocho' (SW 8th Street) running east from 37th Avenue. More than a quarter of Greater Miami's 2 million people are Cubans, and here is where they hand-roll their cigars, eat wonderful food, and dance.

Try the strong Cuban coffee, served espresso-style on the street in paper cups, or cocoa for dipping your *churro* (a long thin doughnut). At Ocho and 14th Avenue is the site of the open-air **Domino Park**, where neighborhood enthusiasts (male only, women just watch) play chess with a concentration worthy of a grand master. The **Manuel Artime Theater** (900 SW 1st Street) is home to the **Miami Hispanic Ballet**. On Ocho and 12th Avenue is **El Crédito Cigar Factory**, where you can watch cigars being rolled, pressed, wrapped, and cut with elegant dexterity. Round off your visit in one of the terrific Cuban restaurants which line the streets.

The closest thing Miami has to an artists' quarter is **Coconut Grove** (South Bay Shore Drive), which is a pleasant self-contained community of boutiques, galleries, and parks, with stylish sailing boats bobbing in the harbor. Coconut Grove and South Beach are the two places to stay if you don't want to have to rent a car. Both neighborhoods also have lots of nightlife, which cannot be said for the rest of the town.

Across the Rickenbacker Causeway, **Key Biscayne** has delightful beaches at Bill Baggs Cape Florida State Recreation Area. But the star of Miami's many wildlife attractions is the **Miami Seaquarium** (tel: 305-365-2501; www.miamiseaquarium. com), just off the causeway on Virginia Key. Here you'll find whales, dolphins, sharks, and turtles at play, eating, and in languid repose. The dolphins leap any height for a few fish and the spectators' delight. A recent and popular addition is the chance to swim with the dolphins. Seaquarium is also one of the few places where you can see the rare manatee, or sea cow, a large

A talented dolphin show at the legendary Seaquarium

seal-like mammal that used to live in great numbers in Florida's waterways. In **Parrot Jungle**, on Jungle Island (www.jungleisland.com), the birds perform more tricks than the dolphins – riding bicycles, roller-skating, even doing arithmetic. The flamingos alone are worth it.

But people are the most fascinating tricksters. Look at what industrialist James Deering did with his **Vizcaya** home (3251 South Miami Avenue; tel: 305-250-9133; www.vizcayamuseum.org). This opulent, 70-room Renaissance-style *palazzo* on Biscayne Bay displays almost every artistic style that Western man produced, from the AD200 altar to the 1915 gold plumbing fixtures. The formal gardens are bizarrely beautiful and the barge in the harbor is made of stone, a sculpture by A. Stirling Calder, less mobile than the works done later by his son Alexander. An afternoon spent here really is a treat.

In 1925, **St Bernard's Monastery** (16711 West Dixie Highway, off Biscayne Boulevard) was shipped from Segovia in Spain – stone by numbered stone – in 11,000 crates. It had been bought by William Randolph Hearst, who intended to use it to house a swimming pool on his estate in California (see page 179). Unfortunately, the crates were packed with hay that the US Department of Agriculture deemed a health hazard to animals (there had been foot-and-mouth disease in Segovia), so the dismantled monastery stayed on the East Coast. Bought and reassembled by a local entrepreneur, it is now a popular place for weddings. The choral recitals are a deliciously anachronistic experience.

Lastly, the **Holocaust Memorial** (Meridian Avenue and Dade Boulevard) features a sculptural tribute to the Holocaust's 6 million victims, *The Sculpture of Love and Anguish*. Forged by sculptor Kenneth Treister, this devastating 42ft (13m) high bronze arm bears an Auschwitz tattoo number and smaller bronze figures scaling its surface. Combining historical exhibits, photographs, and other sculptural monuments, the memorial prompts an elegiac moment of quiet reflection.

The Everglades (FLORIDA)

The watery plain known as the Everglades (toll road south to Homestead, then take State Route 27; follow signs to the National Park) has given swamps a good name as wonderlands of natural beauty. A 50-mile (80km) band of brackish water from Lake Okeechobee flows lazily through Florida to the ocean. Called the 'River of Grass,' the slow-moving bog teems with wildlife. **Everglades National Park** (www.nps.gov/ever) covers nearly half a million acres (more than 200,000 hectares) under the protection of US Rangers. The rangers, stationed at visitor centers throughout the park, advise on how to enjoy – and not spoil – the wilderness.

From the park entrance southwest of Homestead (pick up a map at the **Ernest Coe Visitor Center**; tel: 305-242-7700), the road runs 38 miles (61km) to the western Gulf Coast. Marked turnoffs take you to campgrounds and picnic areas beside lakes or near 'hammocks' – raised areas in the swamps. The first turnoff leads to **Royal Palm**, on the edge of a freshwater slough. In the clear waters of the pond you can see shoals of fish, among them the Florida garfish, enjoyed by alligators. You can watch one of the short slide shows at the Visitor Center before taking the Anhinga and Gumbo Limbo foot-trails.

The Anhinga Trail's raised boardwalk circles over sawgrass marsh where you can see alligators, egrets, herons, and the snake-bird. The Gumbo Limbo is a circular half-mile track through jungle vegetation. Watch for raccoons, opossums, tree snails, and lizards, which are very common around these parts.

At the **Shark Valley** Visitor Center (tel: 305-221-8776), you can rent bicycles or take a guided tram tour. The main road ends at **Flamingo**, a former fishing town on a shallow bay dotted with islands. In the good old days, it produced illicit 'moonshine' alcohol; now it caters to tourists with a Visitor Center (tel: 239-695-2945) and a campground. There used to be a motel and cabins at Flamingo, but these were destroyed by Hurricane Katrina in 2005.

Find your own way up to **Everglades City** through a chain of lakes and rivers called 'The Wilderness Waterway.' The abun-

Exploring the Everglades

dant wildlife on the coast and in the interior includes ibises, os-preys, white herons, bald eagles, snowy egrets, otters, roseate spoonbills, green turtles, manatees (the gentle 'sea cows' increasingly threatened by fast motorboats), and rare Florida panthers. Coat yourself in insect repellent and be sure to follow the rangers' advised precautions about poisonous plants and snakes. The Gulf Coast Visitor Center (tel: 239-695-3311) in Everglades City can advise on restaurants and lodging.

The Gold Coast (FLORIDA)

The 70-mile (113km) long Gold Coast north of Miami offers half a dozen vacation resorts favored by those escaping the winter rigors of New York, New England, the Midwest, and Canada. Hotels and condominiums gleam white across wide, palm-tree-lined boulevards that border spotless beaches.

Fort Lauderdale: The peak moment of madness in this town is the month-long Easter vacation when sun-starved students from the north descend. Early evening, teenagers cruise their cars bumper to bumper up and down the A1A 'Strip' along the seafront. Although cheap flights to the Bahamas mean Fort Lauderdale is not as crammed and crazy as it used to be, you still may choose to stay here at a different time. In summer and winter the town settles down, as private boats and yachts (estimated to number 30,000 on and off the canals) drift along the network of inland waterways past elegant marina homes. The best way to view them is to take a paddleboat cruise.

Boca Raton: This elegant town is the winter home of a highly regarded polo club, but you can also enjoy the wonderful beaches tucked behind the dunes. Or rent a rod and pretend to fish off the rocks around the inlet. If you must be active, go birding or hiking around Deerfield Island Park, once the home of Chicago mobster Al Capone.

Norton Museum of Art, Palm Beach

Palm Beach: The place that put the 'gold' in the Gold Coast. (The palms in Palm Beach are said to have grown from coconuts spilled in a Spanish shipwreck.) The town was created after oil and railroad magnate Henry Flagler was persuaded at the end of the 19th century that Florida's warm winters made the state a viable proposition for his railroad expansion. At the same time as the railroad was being built down the Gold Coast, the secluded location of Palm Beach struck Flagler as just the kind of place for his kind of person. Now one of America's wealthiest communities, it stretches its splendid *palazzi* along Ocean Boulevard, not far from the proprietors' yachts in the harbor. You can catch glimpses of these opulent residences as you wind through the impeccable landscaping. Flagler's own home is on Coconut Row, a white marble palace named Whitehall, is now the **Flagler Museum** (tel:

561-655-2833; www.flaglermuseum.us). Its 55 opulently restored rooms trace the town's early history amid elegant old furnishings, including the master's private railway car. The **Norton Museum of Art** (tel: 561-832-5196; http://norton.org) has a splendid collection of French Impressionists and post-Impressionists.

In this, Florida's ultimate consumer paradise, there is scarcely a luxury store of the world not represented on **Worth Avenue**, a street that ranks alongside Paris's Rue du Faubourg St-Honoré or London's Bond Street. Even if your budget doesn't allow you to go wild, you can still press your nose against the windows. The Gucci store is worth the detour – it's nothing less than a Florentine *palazzo*, with fountains playing in the tree-shaded courtyard.

Kennedy Space Center: Located about 100 miles (160km) to the north on Merritt Island, the Kennedy Space Center (tel: 321-944-4444; www.kennedyspacecenter.com) is America's busiest rocket and Space Shuttle launch facility. There's certainly plenty to see. Four tours (some require advance reservations) and many attractions are on offer. These include walk-through exhibits on exploration and early space travel; the space station module; robotic space explorers; the *Apollo-Soyuz* command module; the moon rocket; interactive space flight simulators; the launch status ('mission control') center, and two IMAX theaters. Unlike Disney, this is an actual working facility, so you may be lucky enough to witness a real space launch.

The Magic Kingdom

Orlando *(FLORIDA)*

Walt Disney World Resort

(20 miles/32km southwest of Orlando off Interstate 4 and State Highway 192. For more information, including Disney's wide range of accommodations, tel: 0870-2424-900, or go online at http://disney world.disney.go.com): Walt Disney World has its own hotels, campgrounds, golf courses, water theme parks, boating facilities, vacation villas, and stores, surrounding some of the biggest theme parks in the world. The area covers 43 sq. miles (111 sq. km) – much of it reclaimed marshland.

Unless you have bought a package that includes entrance fees, you can choose between an annual ticket and a myriad of other types of ticket, from one-day to a week or more. The days don't have to be consecutive, and once you're inside, all rides and exhibits are free. A 'Fastpass' ticket cuts down on the excruciatingly long waiting lines. At each park entrance, be sure to pick up a map and a timetable.

The Magic Kingdom: Once past the ticket booths, choose between the ultra-modern monorail or the more leisurely ferryboat across the lake to the Magic Kingdom's entrance. Now you're in fairyland, with Cinderella's castle, and surrounded by Mickey Mouse and a host of Disney movie characters. Take your choice of the Kingdom's many different sections.

Main Street, **USA**, is the symbol of the good old American way of life, from the entrance under the Train Station past gabled and turreted turn-of-the-19th-century buildings to Town Square, where City Hall dispenses information about the rest of the Magic Kingdom and Walt Disney World in general.

Adventureland proposes exotic tropical flora and fauna. A gigantic (concrete) banyan tree supporting the Swiss Family Robinson Treehouse stands by the landing stage for the Jungle Cruise, complete with trailing vines and (foam-rubber) wild animals. Pirates of the Caribbean trades on the wildly popular movies of the same name, where buccaneers fire cannons, chase wenches, squabble over booty, and quaff beer on overhead bridges. Frontierland romanticizes the pioneer days. Splash Mountain is a log flume ride with a drenching finale, while Big Thunder Mountain Railroad is a roller coaster in an elaborate red-rock setting. The Frontierland Shootin' Arcade is where for a few quarters you can take target practice with old-fashioned rifles that emit laser beams instead of bullets.

Liberty Square doesn't quite replace a visit to New England but makes a valiant effort to capture the atmosphere of the Republic's cradle at Liberty Tree Tavern. The big attraction, though, is the Haunted Mansion.

Fantasyland takes you on a dizzying whirl in the Mad Hatter's gigantic teacup. Every childhood character seems to be here, including Peter Pan and Snow White's Seven Dwarfs. Among Fantasyland's most winning attractions is Mickey's Philhar-Magic, a 3-D show presented continuously throughout the day in a 500-seat theater, where Donald Duck guides you through a world of 3-D animation, music, and special effects.

Mickey's Toontown Fair is a 3-acre (1-hectare) extravaganza with sections devoted to Goofy, Minnie, and the main mouse, Mickey. Check out the interactive lily pads.

Tomorrowland is devoted to space technology and sci-fi. What the Tomorrowland Indy Speedway has to do with the future is a mystery, as it is essentially a go-kart ride, but very popular. More dynamic is Buzz Lightyear's Space Ranger Spin, where every car is equipped with a joystick, laser cannons, and electronic scoreboards.

The idea is to help Buzz save the universe from the evil Emperor Zurg by blasting as many bad guys as possible.

Epcot Center: The Experimental Prototype Community of Tomorrow is south of the Magic Kingdom. The park presents the past and future of our planet, all within a few hundred acres around an artificial lake. Mission: SPACE is a fantastic ride. Honey, I Shrunk the Audience is a crowd-pleasing 3-D movie loaded with special effects. World Showcase offers crib notes and cuisine to travelers unable to trek the globe. And IllumiNations, Epcot's pyrotechnic extravaganza, is a spectacle unlike anything you are likely to have seen elsewhere.

In **Future World**, a monorail takes you around polygonal, spherical, dome-shaped, or pyramidal pavilions (each sponsored by a major American company) demonstrating the evolution of our civilization and the new technologies that will be tomorrow's tools. The centerpiece is Spaceship Earth, a 180ft (55m) high, white geosphere. Other attractions include the **Universe of Energy** and the **Wonders of Life**, including Body Wars, a simulator ride that sends you on a frenetic journey through the human body. The other part of Epcot is **World Showcase**, which presents different nations through their monuments, landmarks, and cuisines.

Enjoying the Disney magic

Disney's Hollywood Studios: The Art Deco streets of this theme park lead to real and replica film sets. You'll see extreme stunt shows, ride through movie history, meet the Muppets in 3-D, and learn some of the secrets of Walt Disney's animation techniques. The Rock 'n' Roller Coaster Starring Aerosmith has cars that look like limousines, each equipped with a sound system blasting an Aerosmith tune.

The big draw around **Echo Lake** is the Indiana Jones Epic Stunt Spectacular. Fastasmic! is a nightly show that dazzles the audience with lasers, fountains, and fireballs.

Disney's Animal Kingdom: This park, the largest of all the parks, is essentially a state-of-the-art zoo dressed up in extravagant style. As well as live shows like the Festival of the Lion King, based loosely on the animated film, there are nature walks where you can view endangered species like black-and-white colobus monkeys, hippos, gorillas, and meerkats.

To see some of the highlights of all the parks, you'll need at least a week, maybe even more. You'll walk miles

Jurassic Park recreated at Universal

and miles, and there's a lot of waiting in line when the parks are at their busiest. This is particularly tiring on a hot summer's day (the most popular months are June to August), although you can rent strollers (pushchairs) and wheelchairs.

Universal Studios Orlando (tel: 407-363-8000): Film and TV fans can relive some of their favorite movies and see new productions in progress. Hundreds of millions of dollars have been spent to create thrilling special-effects rides – based on movies, of course, like *Revenge of the Mummy* and *Men in Black*. Some real, some look-alike stars make an appearance, as does Shrek – in 4-D. Make sure you arrive early in the day in order to find out about any special events that might be planned. You'll need to spend most of the day here: one- and two-day tickets are available. There's a lot of walking, though strollers and wheelchairs can be rented. **Island of Adventure** is another Universal theme park, with no direct movie tie-ins. Instead, five elaborately themed zones are arrayed around a central lagoon. Cutting-edge rides, including two of the best steel roller coasters on the East Coast, keep hardened thrill-seekers happy, while gentler attractions like those at Seuss Landing – inspired by the work of the children's book author – enchant kids.

Elsewhere in the South

Charleston (SOUTH CAROLINA): Standing aloof at the point where the Ashley and Cooper rivers flow together into the Atlantic Ocean, this town evokes that elegant, courtly atmosphere that people still associate with the 'Old South.' After South Carolina led the Southern States' secession from the Union, Charleston was the town that fired the first shots in the Civil War. Ever since, it has maintained, with winning self-consciousness, the South's distinctively well-mannered sense of dignified separateness.

Charleston's Historic District includes over 2,000 buildings. You might start at **The Battery**, curving up to East Bay Street, where antebellum houses snake along narrow shaded cobblestone streets surrounded by gardens of dogwood, wisteria, and azalea. Running west from East Bay Street is Market Street, which leads to attractive **Market Square**. Here, open-air cafés, restaurants, art galleries, and boutiques have been installed in renovated warehouses. It's a great place to have lunch, and watch the people and the workings of this charming city.

From the Municipal Marina at the junction of Calhoun Street and Lockwood Drive on the west (Ashley River) side of the peninsula, you can take a boat trip out to **Fort Sumter** (tel: 843-883-3123; www.nps.gov/fosu). This is the military base that, during the Civil War, was wrested from the United States Army by the South Carolina militia in April 1861, to the polite applause of the Charleston gentry assembled on the harbor, and effectively began the Civil War. The fort was recaptured by the

Union army nearly four years later. An organized two-hour boat cruise usually includes a visit to the Civil War Museum and a tour of the remains of the fort.

Two excursions out of town will take you back to the ante-bellum days of the cotton plantations. **Boone Hall** (7 miles/ 11km north on Highway 17; tel: 843-884-4371; http://boonehall plantation.com), a restored 18th-century plantation home and grounds, is said to have been the inspiration for Tara Plantation in the movie *Gone with the Wind*. Even more spectacular grounds are at beautiful **Magnolia Plantation and Gardens** (tel: 800-367-3517; www.magnoliaplantation.com), located 14 miles (23km) north of Charleston on Highway 61. This lovely 400-acre (160-hectare) site combines a tour of the house with exotic flora and fine opportunities to im-merse yourself in nature by taking the tram tour.

Atlanta's soaring skyline

Atlanta (*GEORGIA*): The historic capital of Georgia is also the bold and busy capital of the New South. The town's sym-bol, which you can see in two fine sculptures – one on Broad Street by the First National Bank, the other on Martin Luther King Drive – is the phoenix, the mythical bird that rose from its own ashes. The town's modern prosperity was spurred by its total destruction in 1864 during the Civil War. Two years later it was the fed-eral headquarters for the South's Reconstruction, and its dynamism is still intact.

Venue for the 1996 Olympic Games, the town has brave contemporary architecture, elegant stores, smart restaurants, and lively nightclubs. To get an ideal overview, start your tour with a trip to the 70th-floor revolving restaurant on top of the (Westin) **Peachtree Plaza Hotel** – the elevators whiz up through glass tubes on the outside of the building. The view is spectacular: on a clear day you can see all the way to the Blue Ridge Mountains in North Carolina.

Linked to the plaza, **Peachtree Center** is an airy shopping and business center with attractive landscaping among the skyscrapers, drooping vines and tropical plants, reflecting pools, and splashing fountains. Even if you're not staying there, be sure to visit the Hyatt Regency Hotel; it was a pioneer in modern atrium architecture.

Underground Atlanta is an entertainment complex in the heart of Downtown, with eight different clubs catering to different musical tastes.

The **High Museum of Art** (Peachtree and 16th streets; tel: 404-733-4400; www.high.org) is a stunning white building with a good collection of American decorative art, African art, and fine modern paintings. Its folk art and photography collections are worth a look, too. The High presents excellent touring exhibitions from London, Paris, and China.

Atlanta is the home base of Coca-Cola, and the company's family-friendly **World of Coca-Cola** (121 Baker Street NW; tel: 404-676-5151; www.woccatlanta.com) gives a fascinating glimpse into the history and advertising of this bubbly symbol of Americana. Free drinks are offered, and there's a good gift shop. The dazzling new premises of the World of Coca-Cola, combined with its next-door neighbor, the highly regarded **Georgia Aquarium** (tel: 404-581-4000; www.georgia aquarium.org), brought a new lease of life to this particular part of the city.

Atlanta is also home to CNN-TV, and 55-minute tours (tel: 404-827-2300; reservations recommended) of the studios at the gigantic **CNN Center** on Marietta Street provide fascinating glimpses into a newsroom in full swing, broadcasting to up to 2 billion people worldwide.

The **Martin Luther King, Jr National Historic Site** (Auburn Avenue NE; www.nps.gov/malu) is Atlanta's most moving experience. The large site includes several facilities: the Visitor Center (at No. 450) features exhibits from MLK's life and the progress of the Civil Rights movement; the King Center (No. 449) is an institute for social change, where MLK's tomb is located; the Ebenezer Baptist Church (No. 407) is where MLK and his father preached their message of non-violence. The King Birth Home can be visited on a guided tour.

New Orleans (*LOUISIANA*): Whatever is exotic, even sinful in the popular image of the South stems in large part from this port town at the mouth of the Mississippi River. In New Orleans, the jazz that grew up in its brothels and steamy saloons is still hot, and the Creole cooking brought from the West Indies by the old French and Spanish settlers even hotter. You'll find them both in the French Quarter. And if the elegant decadence of the antebellum aristocracy is at best a whispered legend handed down to a few strutting diehards, take a look at their granddaddies' splendid Greek Revival townhouses in the Garden District and you'll see what a proud

Making music in New Orleans's French Quarter

Refreshment at Mardi Gras

world they inhabited. August 2005 saw around 80 percent of New Orleans submerged by flood waters, following the damage to the defensive levees caused by Hurricane Katrina. However, much of what makes New Orleans unique was untouched (the French Quarter and the Garden District, being the oldest parts of New Orleans, are located on high ground,) and the spirit of the city remains intact.

New Orleans is well known for its great Mardi Gras carnival (usually February or March), so successful that the city fathers are now turning every imaginable occasion – Halloween, St Patrick's Day, the arrival of spring or summer – into another festival, however hot and humid it may get. The city loves parades, but if they haven't found an excuse for one when you're visiting, you'll still find a public party going on somewhere, and with all the trumpets and trombones blowing full blast, it won't be hard to find.

French Quarter: Known locally as the Vieux Carré (Old Square), this is the historic heart of town, bounded by Canal and Rampart streets (the latter originally a fortification), Esplanade Avenue, and the Mississippi River. Great fires in 1788 and 1794 destroyed over 1,000 houses in the quarter, but rebuilding in the 19th century produced the two- and three-story houses with filigreed wrought-iron galleries that we see today.

Start at **Jackson Square**, where, around the statue of General Andrew Jackson, there is bustle all day long with magicians, balloon-vendors, and assorted eccentrics sporting strange costumes. Flanking the cathedral are two handsome relics of the colonial era – the **Cabildo**, originally a police station and later the City Hall, and the **Presbytère**, a priests' residence that became a courthouse. They are now part of the **Louisiana State Museum** (tel: 504-568- 6968; http://lsm.crt.state.la.us). The Cabildo's exhibits tell the often exciting history of trade on the Mississippi, while the Presbytère houses cultural displays that aptly illustrate the area's rich history through the use of photographs and maps.

St Louis Cathedral is an 1851 restoration of the 18th-century church of the French Catholic diocese, more famous for the duels in its garden than for its architecture. Around the square are the elegant rows of the **Pontalba Buildings**, with wrought-ironwork on the upper-story galleries.

Walk down Dumaine Street past **Madame John's Legacy**, a preserved French colonial cottage, to Royal Street, one of the most gracious in the quarter, awash with high-class antiques shops. To the right, at 1132 Royal Street, the **Gallier House**, named after its architect, James Gallier, is open to the public. It has been restored to its original 1857 condition, and if you walk out on the

Mardi Gras

Shrove Tuesday, the British call it, but people in the United States use the French and know it as 'Fat Tuesday,' a last hedonistic fling before Lenten austerity. It's New Orleans's great moment of madness, bringing thousands of revelers – be sure to book your hotel room well in advance – for the parade of floats down St Charles Avenue, and others throughout the city. The King of Rex, the star of the main and most popular parade, is a local businessman, while the King of Bacchus, whose parade is two days earlier, is always a celebrity.

Private masked balls start on Twelfth Night (January 6), and the parades start 11 days before Mardi Gras. Although Mardi Gras takes place in February or early March, the weather is usually delightfully balmy.

wrought-iron balcony you get a view of the neighborhood's old tranquillity. This is an intellectual respite before venturing out to attack the hurly-burly of **Bourbon Street's** saloons.

If you want to save Bourbon Street till night, hop aboard one of the modern riverfront streetcars for a ride along the Mississippi. *A Streetcar Named Desire*, the play by Tennessee Williams, made this type of local transportation famous. Desire is in fact the name of a street a dozen or so blocks east of here, and that streetcar doesn't run anymore, but you can take a St Charles Avenue streetcar through the Garden District and back starting from Carondelet at Canal. Locals as well as tourists hop on and off these eco-friendly vehicles all day long.

Back in the quarter and close to the waterfront is the **French Market**. Here boutiques and souvenir shops segue into a covered produce and condiment market, alternating with many open-air restaurants providing the theme music of New Orleans – live jazz. The ever-popular 24-hour **Café du Monde** serves delicious *café au lait* and *beignets* (doughnuts), on a very Gallic terrace. The **Riverwalk**, on the site of the 1984 World's Fair

All That Jazz

Cotton is no longer king, but jazz has returned to its throne in New Orleans. The once disreputable music is now officially honored in Louis Armstrong Park on the edge of the French Quarter, and at the New Orleans Jazz National Historic Park; visit the Visitor Center (in the quarter, past Café du Monde) to find out who's playing where. The fabulous New Orleans Jazz and Heritage Festival is one of the largest music festivals in the world (last weekend in April and the first weekend in May).

Jazz began at the end of the 19th century when African-American marching bands played for every social event, especially funerals, and swung all the way home, stopping in at bars and dance halls along the way. Today the action is on Bourbon, Decatur, and Frenchmen streets, shaking that rhythm more loudly than ever.

(other side of Canal Street), is a fine mall complex right on the river.

Garden District: Southwest of the French Quarter, bordered by Magazine Street and Louisiana, St Charles, and Jackson avenues, is the Garden District. This is where the new American cotton and sugar aristocracy built their townhouses after the Louisiana Purchase, while the Creoles stayed on in the Vieux Carré. Sur-

Paddlesteamers still ply the Mississippi River

rounded by gardens of magnolias, oaks, and palm trees, the mansions (most not open to the public) rival outlying plantation homes. There are some particularly fine examples along **Prytania Street**.

The district's golden era ended with the double blow of the Civil War and the elimination of the Mississippi steamboat trade by the railroads. Paddlesteamers still offer **river tours**, starting from the Canal Street docks. Most of the cruises take you past **Chalmette National Historical Park** (also an easy 10-mile/16km drive southeast on Route 46). Andrew Jackson's crushing victory here over the British in 1815 in the Battle of New Orleans came after a peace treaty had been signed, but it was enough to give him the national fame that won him the White House 14 years later.

If you care to end your visit with an antebellum adventure, paddlesteamers set sail several times a day from the wharf at the foot of Canal Street. Cruises can be as brief as a two-hour tour around the area, as delightful as a dinner cruise complete with Dixieland band, or as wicked as a 10-day voyage, which floats along the Mississippi River through beautiful riverports like Natchez and Memphis all the way to St Louis, Missouri, in the Midwest.

THE MIDWEST

The Midwest, popularly known as the Heartland, is the industrial and agricultural core of the US. From the Great Lakes across the prairies to the Great Plains, the Midwest is dominant in dairy and pig farming, corn and wheat, but it is also an industrial center specializing in steel, rubber, and car manufacture.

Chicago is the transportation hub of the Midwest, main junction for the national railroad system, and today blessed – one might even say cursed – with the world's busiest airport. In the neighboring state of Michigan, it's still an economic truth that if car capital Detroit sneezes, America catches cold. These two cities have achieved their industrial and commercial preeminence with a rich and fascinating ethnic mix that makes them vibrant centers of cultural activity, too.

Chicago (ILLINOIS)

Braced against the shores of Lake Michigan, Chicago is a brash place with a proud urban identity. Often called America's Second City, second that is to New York, this is the birthplace of legends of the Mob, the electric blues, and, reputedly, the pizza. H.L. Mencken called Chicago 'the literary capital of the United States,' and writers from Nelson Algren to Nobel Prize winner Saul Bellow have been keepers of the flame. The Chicago comedy troupe 'Second City Players' spawned Steve Martin, John Belushi, Dan Aykroyd, and the *Saturday Night Live* TV show. Chicago's nickname of the Windy City is attributed to both the filibustering techniques of Chicago politicians (defeating bills by talking them out past their allotted time) and to the boastful promotions for the 1893 Columbian Exposition. The town does also draw very chilly winds from the lake, but that's not how it got its nickname.

A delightful surprise for many first-time visitors is the 15-mile (24km) stretch of sandy beaches and green parkland along the lakefront of this resolutely commercial city. Unlike other cities on the Great Lakes, Chicago reserved most of the land along the lakeshore for parks and residential neighborhoods, and did not allow factories. This means plenty of opportunities to sunbathe, swim, or fish, just a few blocks from the major centers of town.

The city that showed the world how to build skyscrapers learned the technique from necessity. In 1871, a fire swept through the largely wood-built town – scarcely 30 years old – leaving 100,000 homeless. Chicago had to rebuild in a hurry, with new fireproof structures making maximum use of available ground space. The architects who worked out how to construct a building around a metal skeleton, so that it could 'go as high as you like' but with elegance and style, became collectively known around the world as the Chicago School.

They included Louis Sullivan, Daniel Burnham, and, later, Mies van der Rohe. Frank Lloyd Wright also worked in the Chicago area, but is better represented by his residential architecture.

The population of Chicago was recorded as just under 3 million in a 2007 census – a big city by any standards, but still

Chicago Thanksgiving Parade is a lively affair

a long way behind New York, giving an occasionally defensive air to the 'Second City,' but also acting as a spur to achievement. It was inevitable that the town's proud architectural tradition would prompt it one day to build something higher than New York's pinnacles and, sure enough, the Sears Tower held rank as the world's tallest building until it was outdistanced in 1996 by the Petronas Towers in Kuala Lumpur, Malaysia.

The Chicago Symphony is one of the world's great orchestras and the Art Institute is a museum of international renown. But the people themselves, rather than aspiring to the sophistication of Manhattanites, have a distinctively warm and cheerfully sardonic attitude to life that makes them much more approachable in public places. The old image of gangland machine-gunnings is hard to live down, but you'll not find any monuments to Al Capone, and the Mafia is no more influential here than in any other wealthy American city. There's an Anglo-Saxon business establishment, but the public tone is set much more by the Irish, Polish, German, Italian, African-American, and Jewish segments of the population.

The Chicago Transit Authority (CTA) runs a very efficient bus system, and taxis are not too expensive, but for once we recommend renting a car to move around the city, except in the congested Downtown area, if you're staying more than a day. Orientation is easy: the city center is known as the Loop, after the elevated railroad track that loops around the Downtown business district immediately south of the Chicago River. The other neighborhoods are defined in geographical relation to the Loop – North Side, South Side, and West Side.

Michigan Avenue: Instead of starting in the hurly-burly of Downtown, we suggest you first take stock of the city from its most elegant street, certainly busy, but more measured in its pace. Chicagoans call the tree-lined stretch north of the Loop and the river up to Oak Street the **Magnificent Mile**. It contains the town's smartest high-fashion boutiques, jewelry stores, department stores, art galleries, and bookstores. Its image is such that when McDonald's (corporate headquarters: Chicago) wanted to open a branch here, neighboring merchants insisted that the decor be appropriate to the location.

The dominant landmark is the gigantic black-steel 100-story **John Hancock Center** with its dramatic exterior – a diagonally strutted skeleton. This is a vertical street unto itself, soaring 1,107ft (337.5m) into the air. The first five floors are taken up with stores, then there are half a dozen floors for parking, and above that the building has offices and apartments, with a supermarket and a swimming pool for the residents. From the 94th-floor observatory you have a view across to the Michigan shores of the lake, down over the Loop to the steel mills of Indiana, up the lakefront toward Wisconsin, and out across the flat residential neighborhoods of the West Side.

One block west of North Michigan, **Rush Street** is a lively entertainment area with outdoor cafés, nightclubs, restaurants, and taverns that come alive after dark. At Chicago Avenue and Michigan is a strange white-limestone turret that is, in fact, a historic monument, the **Water Tower**. It was built in 1869 to house a pumping station to take water from the lake, and was the only public building to survive the Great Chicago Fire. Today it is surrounded by a pleasant park.

Water Tower Place (845 North Michigan) is an attractive shopping center with waterfalls playing alongside the escalators that carry you up seven floors of stores and restaurants. Four blocks south, **Ontario Street** is 'gallery row' and has a thriving contemporary art scene.

Just before you reach the river, you might pause to take a view of one of the city's more bizarre skyscrapers. The cathedral-like

Tribune Tower has remarkable pseudo-Gothic pinnacles and porch, and 30 stories in between them. Built in 1925 for the *Chicago Tribune* newspaper, it was the successful entry in America's most famous architectural competition. Many of the world's leading architects – a total of 233 entries from 23 countries – submitted designs, with the Bauhaus master Walter Gropius and the great Finnish designer Eero Saarinen among the unsuccessful entrants. Having persuaded the world by default that modern buildings should henceforth have modern designs, the tower became a unique and even lovable eccentricity.

There is an excellent ensemble view of the varied skyscraper styles around the vicinity of the Chicago River from **Michigan Avenue Bridge**. The white terracotta, clock-towered building just north of the bridge is the **Wrigley** of chewing-gum fame, which is particularly attractive when floodlit at night.

West along the river are the twin towers of **Marina City**, resembling two huge corncobs. The circular concrete towers, with

Chicago, home of skyscrapers

apartments shaped like slices of pie on the upper floors, go all the way down to the river's edge. They provide mooring spaces for 500 residents' boats, or the businesspeople who commute to work by motorboat from the lake's North Shore suburbs. Providing a stark contrast behind them is the black-steel-and-glass monolithic slab of Mies van der Rohe's landmark **IBM Building**.

The Loop: With the 'El' (elevated railroad) rattling around its periphery of Wabash Avenue, Lake, Wells, and Van Buren streets, the Loop means business. LaSalle Street, the heart of the financial and banking district, has the same canyon-like quality as New York's Wall Street. The major Downtown department stores are on State Street and Wabash Avenue. One of them was Carson, Pirie & Scott, a mecca for architectural scholars attracted, like the earliest shoppers in 1904, by Louis Sullivan's incredibly intricate ironwork ornament over the Madison Street entrance, as well as by the then-revolutionary horizontally elongated windows. Sadly, Carson's closed in 2007.

The most successful feature of Chicago's business district is the space devoted on its many open plazas to monumental modern sculpture and mosaics rather than statues of famous men. This **plaza art**, as it has become known, began with Picasso's great *Sculpture* (1967) in front of the Richard J. Daley Center

Bar Talk and the Great Fire of 1871

It has been established that the Great Fire of Chicago began in the stable of Patrick and Catherine O'Leary over on the West Side on the evening of October 8, 1871. Then Chicago bar legend takes over to insist – and it's not wise to question stories told in a Chicago bar – that it was all the fault of Mrs O'Leary's cow kicking over a paraffin lamp. At any rate, history does record that the fire raged for 27 hours, wiping out over 17,000 buildings, and when a rainstorm put it out, not only was the Water Tower still standing, but – fact, not legend – so was Mrs O'Leary's stable.

(Washington and Dearborn streets), a complex of courthouse and local government buildings named after the late mayor. Like the elegant skyscraper courthouse, the 50ft (15m) sculpture is made of CorTen steel that weathers to the color of rust, but without the corrosion. To people who want to know whether the sculpture is to be understood as a woman or a horse, Picasso himself said they might just

The 'El' winds through the Loop

as well 'try to understand the song of a bird.' At any rate it draws to the plaza a constant flow of admirers and locals who just like to eat their sandwiches around it.

Other notable pieces of plaza art are Chagall's *Four Seasons*, a 70ft (21.5m) long mosaic on the First National Plaza (Monroe and Dearborn streets); a 53ft (16m) high bright red *Flamingo Stabile* by Alexander Calder (Adams and Dearborn streets), gracing what is regarded by some as the most elegant set of US Government buildings in the country, the **Federal Center**, designed by Mies van der Rohe; and, perhaps the most provocative, pop artist Claes Oldenburg's filigreed *Batcolumn*, a 100ft (30.5m) high baseball bat made of 1,608 pieces of welded steel (just outside the Loop at the Social Security Administration Building, 600 West Madison Street).

On the edge of the Loop is the **Sears Tower** (Wacker Drive and Adams Street, now officially called the Willis Tower), which with its 110 floors rising 1,454ft (443m) in the air, was once the tallest building in the world. Actually the building consists of nine towers packed together, as its designers Skidmore, Owings & Merrill suggest, like squared cigarettes; they pop out of their packet at different heights. The structure's steel frame is sheathed in black alu-

Sears Tower

minum with 16,000 bronze-tinted windows. Then there's the 103rd-floor **Skydeck** observatory. If you went up the Hancock in the daytime, try the Sears at night for a great view of the Hancock.

Lake Shore Drive: A trip along the Outer Lake Shore Drive expressway is a delightful way to see the lakefront skyline. On the South Side, you drive from Jackson Park past the sailboats moored in Chicago Harbor at Grant Park, up around Oak Street Beach, to Lincoln Park on the North Side and the boats of Belmont Harbor. South Lake Shore Drive leads to Chicago's greatest concentration of post-millennium architecture, situated in the aptly named **Millennium Park**.

Crown Fountain consists of two glass-brick towers bracketing a shallow granite basin. The faces of a thousand Chicagoans alternate on video screens behind the bricks; about every five minutes, the face on the screen puckers up and 'spits' a stream of water that shoots out of the tower.

The **Jay Prtizker Pavilion**, an outdoor concert venue for free classical music performances, was designed by architect Frank Gehry. The pavilion is framed with wavy sheets of stainless steel that resemble giant ribbons curling away from the stage. Gehry was also responsible for the stainless-steel-sided **BP Bridge**, a sinuous pedestrian pathway.

But Millennium Park's best-loved feature (and Chicago's newest symbol) is the curvaceous, three-story steel sculpture called *Cloud Gate*. Created by Anish Kapoor, its curved, reflective surface makes it a cross between a work of art and a funhouse mirror, and it is affectionately known as '**The Bean.**'

Lincoln Park is worth a separate visit for its zoo. It has a terrific ape house, but better than all the usual tropical exotica (of which there's a good sample) is the charming idea of presenting farm animals – pigs, cows, goats, ducks, and chickens – for city kids who never saw a chicken that wasn't fried or barbecued and know little else besides cats, dogs, and pigeons. Similarly, the **Lincoln Park Conservatory** not only has a beautiful orchid collection and amazing African and South American trees, but also the simple enchantment of hollyhocks, hyacinths, snapdragons, and daisies in Grandmother's Garden.

Museums in Chicago

Museum Point in Grant Park (1300 South Lake Shore Drive) combines three fascinating exhibitions. The **Shedd Aquarium** (tel: 312-939-2438; www.sheddaquarium.org) is one of the largest in the world. It has 7,500 species of fish, including a

Beethoven on the Lawn

Among the Windy City's many achievements, few are more respected than the world-famous Chicago Symphony Orchestra, where the late George Solti was one of a long series of distinguished European resident conductors.

Tickets for their concerts at Symphony Center (220 South Michigan Avenue) are difficult to get, but if you know well in advance when you'll be in Chicago, you can contact the orchestra directly for program details and reservations; go to www.cso.org.

In summer, it's slightly easier to get tickets, when the orchestra plays at Ravinia Park in the northern suburb of Highland Park. Here you can listen to their music and that of other major performers at this summer festival on the lawn while having a traditional 'Ravinia picnic' of chicken, strawberries, and wine.

Inside the Field Museum of Natural History

gorgeous Coral Reef collection of 350 Caribbean creatures. If you're lucky, you'll be there when scuba-divers go down to feed the big fish. The **Field Museum of Natural History** (tel: 312-922-9410; www.field museum.org) also encourages visitors to 'play' with some of the exhibits, though you may be intimidated at first by the giant rogue elephants fighting in the main hall. The **Adler Planetarium** (tel: 312-922-7827; www.adlerplanetarium. org) offers attractive multi-media sky shows. Apart from the well-presented but by now quite usual exhibits about space exploration, a highlight is the display of astronomical instruments dating back to the times when people still believed the earth was flat. The **Museum of Science and Industry** (South Lake Shore Drive and 57th Street; tel: 773-684-1414; www.msichicago.org) is the city's most popular museum because you don't just stand there and look, you get into the exhibits and do things. Go down a coal mine, walk through a huge model of the human heart, creep around a captured World War II German submarine, and press buttons and pull all kinds of levers with scarcely a 'Don't Touch' sign in sight.

The **Art Institute of Chicago** (Michigan Avenue and Adams Street; tel: 312-443-3600; www.artic.edu), at first an art school, now ranks as one of the great American museums. In less than a century it has acquired a collection highlighted by a magnificent range of French Impressionists and post-Impressionists. A new modern wing houses significant works by Matisse, Picasso, Georgia O'Keeffe, and Edward Hopper.

Detriot (MICHIGAN)

Older than Chicago, Detroit was established in 1701 by French aristocrat Antoine de la Mothe Cadillac, whose name is now attached to the aristocrat of General Motors' cars. Detroit became the American capital of car manufacturing after Henry Ford built his first motor-driven vehicle in 1892. He revolutionized the American way of life in 1908 with his mass-produced 'Model T,' which made cars available to everyone.

The centerpiece of the **Renaissance Center** (Jefferson and Brush streets), in the dramatic group of seven shining black-steel-and-tinted-glass towers, is the 73-story, cylindrical **Marriott Hotel**. The vast lobby has an indoor 'lake' surrounded by trees, and the lounges are reached by ramps and spiral staircases. There are bars and a restaurant on the 73rd floor to view the city – and over the border to Canada.

Civic Center continues the Downtown bustle outdoors around **Hart Plaza**, which contains a striking Noguchi fountain. Jefferson Street goes past the **Ford Auditorium** where the Detroit Symphony Orchestra gives its winter concerts.

The **Cultural Center** (around Woodward and Kirby avenues) brings the city's museums together. The **International Institute** (111 East Kirby) assembles under one roof the cultural artifacts, folklore, costumes, and dolls of 50 different countries. The **Detroit Institute of Arts** (tel: 313-833-7900; www.dia.org) has some fine Old Masters, including Pieter Brueghel's *Wedding Dance*, but the most provocative works are the frescoes by Mexican Marxist painter Diego Rivera of Detroit automobile plants. A 2007 renovation of the institute means there are now more than 100 galleries.

Paint it black

A master of the quotable aphorism, tycoon Henry Ford said, 'You can buy my cars in any color you like, as long as it's black.'

THE ROCKIES

The Rockies are a series of mountain ranges extending all the way from Mexico to the Canadian Arctic, running along the great Continental Divide that forms the backbone of America. In Montana, Wyoming, Utah, and Colorado they bring the traveler face to face with the inspiring natural beauties of America's backcountry, its vast forests and torrents, delightful Alpine meadows in summer and wonderful ski slopes in winter.

Formidable barrier to the 19th-century pioneers' westward trek beyond the Great Plains, the Rockies also proved to be a source of great mineral wealth – gold, silver, copper, and, today, uranium.

Fall arrives at Bear Lake, Rocky
Mountain National Park

Yellowstone National Park (WYOMING)

Yellowstone (www.nps.gov/yell), the mountain plateau 8,000ft (2,500m) up in the Rockies, is more than a vast landscape of mountains, valleys, rivers, and forests – both living and petrified. It's a perpetual spectacle of exuberant geysers (including star performer Old Faithful) shooting hundreds of feet into the air, volcanic mudpots exploding, hot springs bubbling out of the earth, and waterfalls so high they make Niagara look like an overflowing bathtub. All of this is set against a backdrop of colors that begin with the yellow of the canyon rock that gives the park its name.

The headquarters for the park are at **Mammoth Hot Springs** on the north side of Yellowstone. Visitors should, if possible, come through the north entrance at Gardiner (Montana Highway 89) or make their way up to Mammoth from the West Yellowstone entrance. The **Visitors' Center** provides tips about campgrounds as well as trail maps, and a museum of the region's flora, fauna, and geological phenomena.

One of the great geological phenomena of the park is at Mammoth: the lovely silver travertine shelves of a **terrace mountain** being created daily before your eyes. Volcanically heated springs are thrusting up mineral-laden water from underground limestone beds and laying their deposits in terraced pools that form at least a couple of tons of new travertine each day.

Drive 21 miles (34km) south of Mammoth to the Norris junction on the 142-mile (230km) **Grand Loop** road that will take you around the major landmarks. An interpretive center at the junction points out short hikes (on boardwalks) across the steaming **Norris Geyser Basin**, and provides good explanations of the workings of geysers and hot springs.

With exceptional luck, you may even witness the world's biggest active geyser, the Steamboat. But unlike that of steady, reliable Old Faithful a little farther down the road, its performance is almost as erratic as a volcano. The spouts vary unpredictably from every few days to just once a year. When it does blow, though, it shoots water, steam, rocks, and mud as high as 400ft (122m) into the air.

Farther south, at Madison Junction, the Loop meets the road from the West Yellowstone entrance and curves down along the Firehole River. This well-named river is fed by hot springs and in places feels like a bath, compared with the plateau streams' chilly 39°F (4°C).

Yellowstone Facts

Most of Yellowstone's 3,472-sq. mile (8,992-sq. km) expanse is in Wyoming, but it also spills over into Montana to the north and Idaho to the west. Only one of the park's entrances, Gardiner, remains open year-round; the others close between November and May. In winter, the park is snowbound and access is only with a rented snowmobile or in the park's own snowbus. Both Salt Lake City and Denver have local airline services to Yellowstone's airport, where you can rent a car. Though all of the major sights can be reached by car, plan on some good walking too.

Lodging must be reserved well in advance, particularly in winter when only the plush Mammoth Hot Springs Hotel and the Old Faithful Snow Lodge & Cabins are open. Access to the Snow Lodge is by park-approved on-the-snow transportation only, and all park lodges are non-smoking. Go to www.travelyellowstone.com for details and to make reservations.

Old Faithful erupts every 65 minutes

Old Faithful, the most famous site in the park, is 16 miles (26km) south of Madison Junction. This is the geyser that you can rely on to blow every 65 minutes or so. Some geysers in the park are larger, but none is as dependable as Old Faithful, which erupts the most frequently of them all. Another Visitors' Center nearby has excellent audiovisual exhibits to explain the phenomenon. This is also the region of three of the park's most active geyser basins, named simply Upper, Midway, and Lower. Be on the lookout, too, for some intriguing, smelly mudpots. These vats of hot, soupy clay are activated by a steam vent, or fumarole.

To escape the crowds that gather at Old Faithful, take the Loop east over to West Thumb (junction with the southern park entrance road, the John D. Rockefeller Memorial Highway) on the shore of beautiful **Yellowstone Lake**. Within strict limitations, you are allowed to fish for cut-throat trout, averaging 18in (46cm). Boats and tackle can be rented either at Grant Village on the lake's southwest tip or at Fishing Bridge on the north shore. Don't forget that you're competing for the fish with otters, osprey, hawks, and grizzly bears, as well as with coyotes hanging around for what others drop.

From the lake's north shore, the Loop follows the Yellow-stone River down to the **Grand Canyon of the Yellowstone**. Approaching from the south, you catch a first sight of the cascading waters of the 109ft (33m) Upper Falls. Park a little farther on near the short trail that will take you to **Inspiration Point**, where you can survey the even more dramatic 308ft (94m) **Lower Falls** and a panorama of the winding 24-mile (40km) long canyon. It drops 1,200 to 4,000ft (360 to 1,200m) to the banks of the Yellowstone River. The canyon walls are impregnated with arsenic sulfides that produce every shade and variation of yellow, wonderfully enhanced by the brilliant greens of the surrounding lodgepole-pine forests.

A Yellowstone resident

At the northern end of the canyon is **Tower Fall** (near the junction with the north-east park entrance road from Cooke City). On a sunny day at noon you'll almost certainly see a double rainbow across the 132ft (40m) high falls. And if you think that the huge perched boulder is about to tumble down, 'discoverers' of the Tower Fall on August 27, 1870, placed bets that it would be gone by the following day.

East of Tower Junction, off the Lamar Valley Road, lies a fascinating **petrified forest**. These solid trees, still upright after millions of years, include sycamores, magnolias, maples, oaks, redwoods, walnuts, and willows – their markings still visible. This suggests that Yellowstone was once a great deal warmer than it is today. The forest was covered by volcanic ash rich in silica with which groundwater impregnated the trees and plants, eventually turning them to stone.

Denver (COLORADO)

If you don't believe Denver was once the mining capital of Colorado, look at the 24-carat gold-leaf dome on its Capitol Building, or at the local branch of the US Mint that handles a quarter of the nation's gold supplies. The Wild West days have long gone, but locals still like to sport a Stetson hat and checked shirt, for old times' sake. The architecture is relentlessly modern, apart from one colorfully preserved street from the old mining days. But what counts is what you see almost on the city's doorstep – the marvelous backdrop of the Rocky Mountains, Denver's backyard.

The **US Mint** (on Colfax) gives free weekday tours of its money-making plant. You can see gold bullion and the counting room, full of the finished product. Also on Colfax is the august **Capitol Building** (East 14th and East Colfax streets). Take the west staircase and stand on the 18th step – that's exactly one mile above sea level.

The best of the modern city is the **Denver Art Museum** (West 14th Avenue and Bannock Street; tel: 720-865-5000; www.denverartmuseum.org). Its seven-story walls are covered with a million glass tiles over a surface broken up higgledy-piggledy with slotted windows, a true architectural spectacle. The museum contains a first-class collection of Native American art – totem poles, costumes, and rugs – as well as changing exhibitions from all areas of world art.

Old Denver is over on **Larimer Street**, which has conserved its Victorian buildings as art galleries, stores, and cafés – some good Mexican restaurants, too. Larimer Square is done up with courtyards and arcades lit by gas lanterns. But the most authentic piece of old Denver is to be found in the grand lobby of the 1892 **Brown Palace Hotel** (17th and Tremont Place), genteel forerunner of the skylit atrium style of today's glass-tower hotels.

From September to May, the Denver Symphony Orchestra plays at **Boettcher Concert Hall** (14th and Curtis streets), an acoustically sophisticated auditorium-in-the-round which, with the audience encircling the performers, provides a unique opportunity to see the conductor's facial expressions. Classical and popular music concerts are held 16 miles (26km) southwest of town in the dramatic, open-air arena of **Red Rocks**, set in the middle of red-sandstone outcrops.

If you don't have time for an extended tour of the Rockies, you can still get a taste of

Gardens galore in Denver

one of the higher mountains by driving all the way to the top. Just west of Denver, **Mt Evans** is 14,260ft (4,346m) high, with a paved road to its peak. (Drive 35 miles/57km on Interstate 70 to Idaho Springs and then south on Route 103 to Route 5.)

Rocky Mountain National Park: Straddling the Continental Divide in north central Colorado, west of and in between the cities of Fort Collins and Boulder, the Rocky Mountain National Park is a wonderland of sky-scraping peaks, 150 lakes, rushing mountains streams, Alpine tundra, pristine forests, and an amazing array of wildlife. The park's highest peak is the 14,255ft (4,345m) **Longs Peak**, which towers over the eastern side of the park and challenges even the fittest of climbers. Another popular destination is **Bear Lake**, nestling beneath Hallett Peak and the starting point for many hiking trails.

West Central Colorado

An ambitious tour of the major resorts of west central Colorado will take you on a beautiful 360-mile (583km) circuit through the Rocky Mountains, but if time is limited you may prefer to aim for just one of the big three.

Aspen: Aspen is the best-known resort town in the state. At 7,937ft (2,419m) it provides wonderful winter-sports opportunities, but it's also a delight in summer, both for its music festival and for the hiking, camping, fishing, and horseback riding in the surrounding **White River National Forest**. In the 1880s the town made its fortune from silver mining, but the market collapsed in 1893 and the town was deserted until revived as a sports and cultural center after World War II. Some of the old Victorian buildings have been preserved with considerable charm and taste, particularly the Opera House and the luxurious Hotel Jerome.

The summertime Aspen Music Festival presents opera, classical music, and jazz of the highest order. International stars like to hang out here. They take advantage of the easygoing atmosphere in the Downtown mall and outdoor cafés or go for

Natural Behavior

Human beings are only guests in America's national wilderness areas, and it is not a good idea to interfere with the residents – the moose, antelope, bighorn sheep, bear, bison, fish, and birds. Under no circumstances should you feed bears. The ferocious grizzlies number about 250 in Yellowstone alone, the black bears about 600. A program to remove the bears from the busiest tourist areas has reduced bear-related injuries, but bears still seek out campgrounds for food.

After being reduced by wanton slaughter in the 19th century from millions to just a few hundred on the whole continent, bison are back in the Rocky Mountain area. National parks' ecological policy of strict non-interference with nature means, for instance, that no attempt is made to save the moose herds from starvation in the bitter winters.

excursions into the spectacular **Maroon Bells** mountains south-west of town. In winter, skiing opportunities vary from the family slopes on Buttermilk and nearby Snowmass to the challenges on Aspen Highlands or Ruthie's Run on Aspen Mountain.

Vail: North of the White River National Forest, this is a successful modern ski resort with Swiss-style chalets. In summer it caters to tennis and golf enthusiasts – the only real problem with the golf course being that the scenery is so spectacular it can easily distract you from your game. Surprisingly, there is also enough gentle landscape around to make cycling a special pleasure. Anglers fish for trout in Gore Creek and Eagle River.

Glenwood Springs: This destination offers the luxury of a 405ft (123.5m) long swimming pool fed by a stream of natural warm water to a temperature of 85–90°F (29–32°C). The waters were much prized by Native Americans as energizers before going on the hunt or warpath. They'll definitely relax you after some exhilarating rafting down the **Colorado River**.

Vail is a skier's paradise

Salt Lake City (UTAH)

A unique phenomenon in American life, Salt Lake City is a community founded and sustained on theological doctrine – that of the Mormons, or, to give them their full name, the Church of Jesus Christ of Latter-Day Saints. It is also an upscale town with bright shopping centers and outdoor cafés as well as impressive monuments to a historic spirit of adventure and courage. In the last half-decade, non-Mormons have discovered the attractions of the city, and the population is growing. All this is carved out of a desert of salt flats that stretches from the foot of the Wasatch Range of the Rockies around the Great Salt Lake all the way across Utah to the mountains of Nevada. This geographical isolation has motivated the people of Salt Lake City to keep up a busy cultural life of ballet, choral music, and art exhibitions.

Temple Square is the all-important center of Salt Lake City, a 10-acre (4-hectare) compound surrounded by a 15ft (4.5m) high wall containing the nucleus of the Mormons' church buildings, including the Temple, Tabernacle, and Visitors' Center. The solid granite Temple, 40 years in the building, is closed to non-believers, but the celebrated **Tabernacle** is open to everyone. Its vast 250ft (76m) long and 150ft (46m) wide turtleback dome, originally made of wood shingles but now encased in aluminum, was constructed only with wooden dowels, no nails, since iron was too scarce in Utah in the 1860s. The dome stands on 44 sandstone pillars at its periphery and provides wonderful acoustics for the famous Mormon Tabernacle Choir. The 375 singers sometimes hold free rehearsals on Thursday evenings. A monumental 11,623-pipe organ enhances the rather stark interior of the Tabernacle.

Beehive House (67 East South Temple) was built in 1854 as the residence of Brigham Young when he served as President of the LDS church and Governor of the Utah Territory. It is now a museum. Rooms, decorated with period furnishings, include the playroom, the fairy castle, and the gracious sitting room, where each evening the Young family sang and prayed together. The life of the early community is portrayed in the **Pioneer Museum**

(300 North Main Street). The **State Capitol**, a copper-domed, Corinthian-style building of Utah granite and marble, affords a sensational view of the Wasatch Mountains.

The **ZCMI** (Zion Co-operative Mercantile Institution) at 15 South Main was one of the country's first department stores, built in 1868. Now its charming, ornate cast-iron facade with slender Corinthian columns, temporarily moved during construction of a $1 billion retail complex, will form the face of a new Macy's store. Similarly, **Trolley Square** (5th South and 7th East streets) has converted old trolley barns for new uses; now they house restaurants, stores, and a theater. (Free motorized trolleys also run to different points around town.) Monday night – the Mormons' Family Evening – is a popular time to visit the ice-cream parlors and movie houses. Salt Lake's strict no-alcohol rules are rapidly being relaxed; you can order a bottle of wine or a cocktail with meals, or become a temporary member of a 'club' and be served a drink.

Mormons

The Mormons' founder, New Englander Joseph Smith, began and ended his religious career with divine revelations. The first, in the 1820s, was that the Native Americans were the Lost Tribes of Israel to be redeemed from paganism by Smith and his followers. Twenty years later, with 15,000 converts in Nauvoo, Illinois, he was directed by revelation to follow the path of polygamy, since the prophet Isaiah had said in the Bible that 'seven women shall take hold of one man.' Smith in fact took 27 wives, and others followed suit until he was shot to death in a conflict with dissidents. Brigham Young succeeded as the Mormons' Prophet, inheriting five of Smith's widows to add to a dozen of his own wives, and led his people on an arduous 1,000-mile (1,690km) trek across the prairies, Great Plains, and the Rocky Mountains to a new promised land. 'This is the place,' were his much-quoted words on surveying the dry expanses of Utah's salt flats. Polygamy remained the official practice until the United States made its disavowal the condition of Utah statehood in 1896.

Salt Lake City's stunning natural setting

Just south of the square, **Liberty Park** makes a lovely picnic ground, with arbors, a swimming pool, a boating lake, an amusement park, and the popular Tracy Aviary. Concerts and festivals are held here in the summer. The **Salt Palace Auditorium** is another venue for concerts and events; on the same grounds, the **Bicentennial Arts Center** is the venue for performances of theater, ballet, and the music of the Utah Symphony Orchestra, with art exhibitions.

You shouldn't leave without a visit to the **Great Salt Lake**. Even if you prefer not to float in its hot, sticky, 25 percent saline water, the sight alone is worth the diversion. The lake, surrounded by marshland and salt flats, is indeed an impressive sight, but much more refreshing is **Wasatch National Forest**, a haven of peace and a pleasure. Opportunities are here for hiking, camping, trout fishing, or fall hunting for deer, moose, antelope, and elk. The area is also a popular destination for winter sports such as skiing and snowboarding, and was the site for the Winter Olympics of 2002.

Monument Valley

THE SOUTHWEST

The region *par excellence* of America's wide open spaces, the Southwest stretches across most of the much-touted American 'Sun Belt.' It covers the vast ranchlands and oil country of Texas, the rugged highlands of New Mexico first settled by the Indians and Spanish conquistadors, and Arizona's deserts rising to pine-forested mountains. Their culmination is the nation's most awe-inspiring sight, a phenomenon that humbles the most blasé of world travelers – the Grand Canyon.

Don't even consider visiting Texas, New Mexico, and Arizona without a car. While buses and planes will take you from town to town, the distances around the towns and between the sights are more than shoe leather or local bus services were meant to deal with. Choose your season well: spring and summer bring the great dry heat of the desert or the humidity and high temperatures of towns like Houston. Come to the region with some of the spirit of the hardy pioneers who settled here.

Dallas (TEXAS)

Television, movies, and the national tragedy of John F. Kennedy's assassination have made this one of the best-known cities in America. The skyline looming out of the plain says it all. The most attractive skyscrapers are the glassy Allied Bank Tower and the gleaming slabs of the Hyatt Regency Hotel. They stand beside **Reunion Tower** (300 Reunion Boulevard, off the Stemmons Freeway). The tower has a revolving cocktail lounge, restaurant, and observation deck for a fine view of the Texas infinity.

The **John Fitzgerald Kennedy Memorial** (Main and Market) is a stark and eloquent monument to the shooting of the president on November 22, 1963. The 30ft (9m) high walls enclose a broken square that is approached along a gently sloping ramp, a space for meditation. The assassination is understandably something the people of Dallas would rather forget, but visitors just won't let them.

Due to public demand, the former Texas Book Depository nearby, from which Lee Harvey Oswald was said to have fired the fatal shots from the sixth floor, has been turned into the **Sixth Floor Museum** (tel: 214-747-6666; www.jfk.org). The museum houses exhibits about JFK's campaign, his social and economic programs, and the space race. Cameras used by spectactors watching the motorcade can be seen, as well as the famous Zapruder camera and some of the footage it recorded of the assassination, the best visual documentation to have surfaced. A videotape of the dramatic events of the day includes a tearful Walter Cronkite (America's most respected newscaster) announcing the president's death.

West of the JFK Memorial is the little **Log Cabin** (Market and Elm), a replica of the one pioneer John Neely Bryan built in 1841 when he came to settle in this part of Texas, the site of the future city of Dallas. The tiny cabin, which was brought here perhaps as a cheerful antidote to the assassination monument, served both as post office and courthouse.

This resolutely forward-looking city has preserved just one area in which it has assembled the remnants of its past – **Old**

City Park (Gano and St Paul streets; tel: 214-421-5141; www.dallasheritagevillage.org). Here you can picnic on the grass among restored Victorian houses, old log cabins, an 1886 railroad depot, a bandstand, turn-of-the-20th-century stores, and a Greek Revival mansion from 1855.

But otherwise, it's the people rather than the buildings that carry the past with them in this town. See them at their best at the **Farmers' Market** (1010 South Pearl), a collection of ramshackle tin-roofed stands where they sell Texas-size fruit and vegetables, chew tobacco, or pick a mean guitar – good ol' boys to a man.

Another local attraction is **Neiman-Marcus** (Main and Ervay), the legendary department store. Nothing is too outrageous for them to sell – solid gold bathroom fittings, pet lion cubs or even His-and-Hers jet aircraft. Neiman-Marcus stores are now located all over America, but these temples to conspicuous consumption started in Texas, of course.

Dazzling Dallas

The free **Dallas Museum of Art** (tel: 214-922-1200; www. dallasmuseumofart.org) is a showcase of treasures money can't buy. But you can view the collection, particularly strong in 19th- and 20th-century art, housed in a landmark building purpose-designed by Edward Barnes.

In the middle of the formidable fanfare of Downtown Dallas, you can easily retreat for a moment's tranquillity in the triangle of **Thanks-Giving Square**, a peaceful little oasis of immaculate lawns, gardens, trees, and channels of water, with a bridge leading to a spiral chapel.

Houston *(TEXAS)*

Houston is oil and space. It's a hot, humid town that has burgeoned into one of the most prosperous business communities in America (though there are some sections of the city that are still struggling). To deal with the heat and humidity, there is an underground network of air-conditioned concourses (fueled by local oil) that link the Downtown skyscrapers.

Oil is proclaimed on its skyline by the striking black wedge-shaped towers of **Pennzoil Plaza**, designed by Philip Johnson, and the gabled, red-granite Republic Bank Center. You can see how the black gold is drawn from the earth at the **Museum of Natural Science** (1 Hermann Circle Drive at Hermann Park). The displays of drilling and refining technology include a model of an offshore oil rig.

The **Museum of Fine Arts** (1001 Bissonnet; tel: 713-639-7300; www.mfah.org) has collections of Indian and pre-Columbian art, while the contemporary art section is a constant source of surprise as wealthy donors bring back new treasures. For local color, the most exciting works on display are the studies of cowboy life by painter and sculptor Frederic Remington. His are the images that have made bucking broncos and gunfighters the icons of the Wild West.

The **Rothko Chapel** (3900 Yupon Street) is a lovely – if somewhat austere – non-denominational place of worship, housing the starkly contemplative purple-and-black canvases of Mark Rothko. The chapel and neighboring **Menil Collection** of art – strong on the Surrealists and on primitive and Asian work – was given to Houston by philanthropists Jean and Dominique de Menil.

About 25 miles (40km) southeast of Houston on Interstate 45, then NASA Road, is the **Johnson Space Center** (tel: 281-483-0123; www.jsc.nasa.gov). This is the controlling hub of the United States space program, where astronauts train and NASA has its monitoring center for manned space flights. The Visitor Orientation Center is a splendid museum of space equipment, rockets, lunar modules, space capsules, and moon rock. Guided tours around the Mission Control Center are given by knowledgeable cadets, and you can also visit the Skylab Training Room, the living and working quarters of NASA's space laboratory.

San Antonio (TEXAS)

For visitors, San Antonio is the most accessible of Texan towns, the historic center of the state's Spanish-Mexican beginnings and delightfully inviting with its River Walk through the heart of Downtown.

The **Alamo** (Alamo Plaza; www.thealamo.org), built as the Spanish Mission San Antonio de Valero in 1718, is the hallowed fortress where 187 Americans fought and succumbed to 5,000 Mexican soldiers under General Santa Ana in 1836. They'd been sent to put down American resistance to Mexico's authoritarian rule of its Texas province. The Americans' heroic stand inspired the revolt which finally won Texas independence and subsequent admission to the US as the Lone Star State.

Today the Alamo is a museum of that momentous battle. Among other memorabilia, it displays the Bowie knife, the curved-bladed weapon fashioned by Colonel James Bowie, joint commander of the Alamo. It was the other commander, William Travis, who issued the order: 'Victory or death.' Best-known of the Alamo heroes was Davy Crockett, who devoted his life to self-promoting acts of courage in Tennessee before being

The Alamo is a symbol of Texas

defeated when he stood in a congressional election. He told his constituents, 'You can all go to hell, I'm going to Texas,' and here he died.

You can see where the Spanish used to rule Texas at the **Spanish Governor's Palace** (tel: 210-224-0601; www.sanantonio.gov), a rather grim edifice dating back to 1749, still emblazoned with the Habsburg eagle of Spain's ruling family over the entrance. The house is furnished with pieces from the Spanish and Mexican eras. You can also see the Mexicans' old adobe houses and stone patios in **La Villita**, the residential neighborhood south of the river along Villita Street. For Mexican shopping, a visit to the old marketplace, El Mercado (515 W. Commerce), is always lively and fun.

The river is San Antonio's pride and joy. The **Paseo del Rio**, or **River Walk**, meanders nearly 3 miles (5km) around a horseshoe curve through town. Below the bustle of traffic, you can walk past banana plants and bougainvillea shading outdoor cafés and ice cream parlors, nightclubs, and craft shops. Water-taxis and river cruises are available at the Market Street Bridge, or dine by candlelight on the pleasure barges. Beyond the river, the water garden of the Paseo del Alamo stretches to the Alamo.

The best museum is the **Hertzberg Circus Collection** (210 Market Street), where working models present a history of the circus from its early days in England to the American heyday of the P.T. Barnum era. Clown costumes, Tom Thumb's dwarf carriage, and a complete circus ring make a nostalgic exhibition.

For a panoramic view of San Antonio and the surrounding country, go out to **HemisFair Park** (tel: 210-207-8572), a relic of the 1968 World's Fair, where there's an observatory on the 652ft (199m) Tower of the Americas. The park is also the site of the Institute of Texan Cultures, devoted to the folklore of the 26 ethnic groups that together have created the state of Texas.

Mission Road running south of town takes you out to the missions that were the basis of Spanish colonization in the 18th century, with Catholic priests converting Native Americans to Christianity while a garrison of soldiers subdued the recalcitrant and searched for gold. **Mission San José** (5 miles/8km south on US Highway 281; tel: 210-922-0543; www.sanjosemission church.org) is the best-preserved of these spiritual and military installations. Founded in 1720, this 'Queen of the Missions' has a Spanish baroque entrance. Inside, you can visit the soldiers' spartan quarters, the granary, and natives' workshops.

Santa Fe (NEW MEXICO)

Founded by the Spanish in 1610, **Santa Fe** is the oldest capital city in the United States. The atmosphere in the historic center of town, for all the invasion of hotels and souvenir shops, still gives a hint of that more leisurely Spanish and Indian era. The rose-colored adobe structures with their *vigas*, log beams holding up the ceilings and roofs, managing miraculously to be both solid and graceful in form, offer their shady arcades as a delightful shelter from the heat of the day.

The **Plaza** is the focus of old Santa Fe. On its north side is the Palace of the Governors, the oldest public building in the US

(1610), now housing part of the **Museum of New Mexico** (www.museumofnewmexico.org), devoted to the history and prehistory of the state. In the arcade along the facade of the palace, Pueblo Indians sell handmade silver and turquoise jewelry (turquoise of fair quality still comes in considerable quantities from the hills of New Mexico). Navajo and international folk art is displayed in annexes of the museums located along the old **Santa Fe Trail**.

Canyon Road, running along the south bank of the Santa Fe River, is the area where the painters, sculptors, and craftspeople have their studios and galleries. Walk in and watch them work. Landscape paintings tend to be intriguing, the ambient color and light being such an inspiration. The **Santa Fe Opera** is housed in a wonderful open-air setting, an amphitheater carved out of the hillside (partially roofed in the unlikely event of rain), 7 miles (11km) north of town on the road to Taos.

Canyon Road is Santa Fe's artistic centre

Taos *(New Mexico)*

Young Native American

In the early 20th century, Taos was an art colony much loved by British novelist D.H. Lawrence. It continues to attract artists and their groupies, who live an easy hand-to-mouth existence just off the town **Plaza**. The town's colorful street life blends society's New Agers with Taos Indians, Spanish-American farmers, and assorted sightseers. Back in the days of Spanish rule, Taos was the center of the Pueblo Revolt (1680) which ultimately lost New Mexico for the Spanish. North of town, the **Taos Pueblo** (tel: 575-758-1028; www.taospueblo.com) is a centuries-old Indian village with 900 residents still inhabiting the sprawling five-story apartment buildings – forerunner of modern America's condominiums. The jewelry, blankets, drums, and baskets sold here make excellent gifts. Visitors are requested to ask before taking pictures of tribe members, and not to wade in the river, as it is the pueblo's only source of drinking water.

At Ranchos de Taos, 4 miles (6.5km) south on Highway 68, the 1772 **San Francisco de Asis Mission** is the most attractive of the adobe churches. A sturdy, buttressed affair, it looks like a massive piece of sculpture.

Phoenix *(Arizona)*

The most spectacular thing about Phoenix is its setting in the **Valley of the Sun**, the perfect backdrop to a Western movie, with the forbidding red Superstition Mountains to the east and towering Camelback Mountain northeast of town.

If passing through Phoenix in the summer, you may find that it's just too hot to get out of your air-conditioned car. However, there are some museums that are worth visiting. The **Heard Museum** (tel: 602-252-8848; www.heard.org) is one of the best of its kind in the country. It traces the history of Native Americans of the Southwest from the first cave-dwellers and Pueblo Indians – with a wonderful collection of Kachina dolls – to modern times.

The **Pueblo Grande Museum** (4619 East Washington; tel: 602-495-0901; www.phoenix.gov/parks/pueblo.html) is an on-site archeological excavation of a Hohokam Indian settlement believed to date back some 2,000 years. The ruins, spread across a broad mound, mark out a civilization that disappeared around the year 1400. As preparation for the flora you'll see on your desert drive, visit the **Desert Botanical Gardens** (tel: 480-941-1225; www.dbg.org), which are 3 miles (5km) east of Pueblo Grande.

Phoenix is a good starting point for the Grand Canyon. There are flights directly up to the canyon from here or, if the prospect of a desert drive appeals, then rent a car here.

The Grand Canyon

No picture, no words will ever match the physical reality of the **Grand Canyon** (www.nps.gov/grca). You'll see it and still won't believe it. That moment will come when you approach the rim of the 277-mile (449km) long, serpentine canyon. Look down to its 1-mile (1.5km) deep floor where the once-mighty Colorado River has eroded a passage and millions of years of earth upheavals have gouged out a theater for the performance of the grand geological drama.

It's always best to avoid the Grand Canyon in the high season of May to September, if possible. There are camping facilities and hotels on the **North Rim**, but that's really for habitués. First-timers should concentrate on the **South Rim**.

Grand erosion

The Grand Canyon was created solely by the erosion of the Colorado River. From the rim of the towering canyon, the river looks like a stream.

Make reservations well in advance if you want to go camping; lodging is also available in **Grand Canyon Village**. Booths at the village provide information about the bus tours of the main **Rim Drive**; cycling around the rim; hiking or riding mules down to the canyon floor; or rafting along the Colorado River. Hiking and mule-riding are for the hardy. Rafting is a spectacular way of seeing the canyon and perfectly safe in the hands of experienced guides.

The **Visitors' Center** at Grand Canyon Village is important for any initial orientation. The rangers here and at key spots along the Rim Drive provide fascinating information on the geology, flowers, animal life, and anthropological history. Especially interesting are the Indians whose dwellings, built into the canyon cliffs, are still visible today on the North Rim.

Up on the rim are fine **nature trails** through forests of juniper and piñon pine. Every now and again you emerge in a clearing on the edge of the canyon to peer down at the giant mounds or buttes rising like Egyptian pyramids or Aztec temples, and bearing such names as Zoroaster Temple or Cheops Pyramid. Some of the other rock formations bear such ominously fanciful names as Skeleton Point and the Phantom Ranch.

Shuttle buses run along the 8-mile (13km) **West Rim** (closed to private cars from May to September), stopping off for wonderful views at Hopi Point, Mohave Point, and Pima Point. Other buses pass frequently and might pick up walkers.

You should attempt to hike only if you are fit and well prepared; although distances are small, the terrain is rough and temperatures are extreme. Wear good walking shoes, a sunhat, sunscreen, and protective clothing, and carry plenty of drinking water.

The easiest route is the **Bright Angel Trail**, leaving from Bright Angel Lodge. Start at daybreak, as you can safely count on a good three hours going downhill, and six or seven hours coming back up. The trail zigzags down 1½ miles (2.5km) to a resthouse (you'll find an emergency telephone installed there), another 1½ miles to the Jacob's Ladder Resthouse, still zigzagging, and then straightening out to the beautiful **Indian Garden** at Garden Creek. You can stay overnight at this ranger station and campground providing you have a reservation, which should be made at least six months in advance.

Stalwart hikers will continue the next morning along Garden Creek around the **Devil's Corkscrew** down Pipe Creek to the River Resthouse beside the Colorado River. With an advance reservation, hikers can also stay at the bunkhouse-style accommodations at Phantom Ranch. A more challenging hike is the steeper **Kaibab Trail** from the Yaki Point Road east of the village.

The hikes take you away from the crowd along the Rim Drive, though even here you can always walk a few hundred yards away and enjoy the beauty of this phenomenon in near-tranquillity.

One of the wonders of the natural world – the Grand Canyon

Nearby Natural Wonders

Grand Canyon West: Just over three hours' drive west of Grand Canyon National Park and two hours' drive east of Las Vegas is this tourist destination with a remarkable attraction – **the Skywalk** – which hovers over the canyon like a ghostly glass footbridge (tel: 877-716-9378; www.grandcanyonskywalk.com). Jutting out over 70ft (21m) from the precipice, the clear view straight down the canyon wall for 4,000ft (1,200m) takes visitors by surprise. Package tours depart from Las Vegas.

Monument Valley: Located around the Utah/Arizona border, this iconic landscape of red sandstone (tel: 928-871-6647; www.navajonationparks.org/htm/monumentvalley.htm) is the crown jewel in the Navajo tribal park system.

A number of Navajo families are licensed to offer horseback and Jeep tours. Fees are usually paid in cash (be sure to tip your guide and any Navajos who pose for photographs).

The dusty, rutted road (impassable after rain) is drivable by passenger cars, but your car will take a pretty serious beating. Take a few bottles of water and allow at least two hours to tour the 17-mile (27km) unpaved scenic drive into the valley.

The **View Hotel** (www.monumentvalleyview.com) is a recently completed low-rise, Navajo-run hotel situated inside the park. Most of its 96 rooms face the most iconic formations, the **Mittens**, while rooms on the top floor are fantastic for stargazing. The hotel is adjacent to Monument Valley's Tribal Park Visitors' Center. Other lodging inside the park includes the 100-site Mitten View Campground. Though basic, this is a great place to see the sun rise behind the carved de Shay sandstone formations.

Bryce Canyon National Park: Thousands of thin, red, weather-carved spires jut out of the canyon floor at Bryce (www.nps.gov/brca) in southern Utah. At 8,000–9,000ft (2,400–2,700m), Bryce is a high-country park, cool in the summer and quietly stunning under fresh snow in winter. An 18-mile (30km) scenic drive winds from the Visitor Center to Yovimpa Point, taking in 13 viewpoints with views to the Colorado River canyons 100 miles (160km) away. Although visitors with cars are allowed, taking the free shuttle is encouraged, in order to preserve the environment.

Most day hikers enjoy the Queen's Garden, Navajo Loop, and Peekaboo Loop trails in **Bryce Amphitheater**, where a fantasia of rock formations delight the senses. Try to be in the park at sunset for Bryce's natural light show, when the color of the rocks turns from red to ochre to darkest purple.

Zion National Park: Still in Utah, visitors to Zion (www.nps.gov/zion) stand at the bottom and peer upward through rock walls so steep that only a sliver of blue sky is visible above.

Along the Zion Narrows Trail

If you're driving, the most dramatic way to approach the park is via the East Entrance. Park at Zion Visitor Center, or in the nearby town of Springdale. Between late March and late October, shuttle buses run from here to the Visitor Center, where other (free) shuttle buses run in a loop that takes in Zion Canyon, the History Museum, Zion Lodge, and trails that link the canyon bottom with the wild rim country beyond.

Zion is particularly beautiful after heavy rain, when waterfalls pour off the rocks at the Emerald Pools or along the short Riverside Walk. This is the terminus of the **Zion Narrows Trail**, a challenging 16-mile (26km) wade/hike. Zion's river trails, lined with dripping springs and verdant hanging gardens of moss, fern, and monkey-flower, offer a cool retreat from the summer heat. Climb the 2½ miles (4km) to **Angels Landing**, a steep trail ending at a heart-stoppingly narrow headland directly above Zion Canyon.

THE WEST

The West is America's most varied playground, catering to the crazy, the lazy, and the easygoing. Only those in search of the hectic are discouraged: here, few people rush. While Las Vegas carries the madness inland to the desert, Seattle on the north-west Pacific Coast introduces a note of sanity in its healthy green state of Washington. But these are the appendages to the American mecca of all dreamers, European and American alike: California. A land blessed with sun and sea and oranges and ice cream, California is quite simply the ultimate fantasy land. Stand on the beach at Malibu, stare out at the Pacific Ocean or back at the Santa Monica Mountains, and every-thing seems possible: balmy winters, shining summers, snow if you want it.

It's no accident that this is the chosen home of America's film industry. California offers every imaginable landscape – Swiss

Living the dream on the West Coast

Alps, Sahara Desert, English meadows, African jungle – all easily accessible from the freeway. And what isn't already here – a Roman forum or Egyptian pyramid – can be built in a few days with the great wealth that California has amassed in little more than a century. Its prosperity is overwhelming and constantly renewed – beginning with the gold of the Sierras, spreading across the great Central Valley to the gigantic combines of agribusiness (mere agriculture was just a passing phase), and

Gun-slinging sheriff

on to the coast for oil and the aerospace industry. Californians are perfectly prepared to work, and work hard, but they can't wait to get back to the tennis court or swimming pool, go surfing in the Pacific or hiking in Yosemite National Park.

Many Californians would like to divide their state into two separate entities: Northern and Southern California – corresponding to two distinct frames of mind represented by San Francisco and Los Angeles respectively. But in fact there's a little bit of both – San Francisco's sophistication and Los Angeles' sunny craziness – all over the state.

This itinerary begins in San Francisco and its nearby wine valleys and works its way down the Pacific Coast to Los Angeles and San Diego before taking off for the national parks of Yosemite, Sequoia, and Death Valley. Whatever routes you choose, if time permits, you should also try to make an excursion to California's favorite out-of-state playground, Las Vegas.

You can get to almost all these places by train or bus, and air travel is relatively inexpensive compared with the rest of the country. However, California is the land of the car, and it will be difficult to enjoy the full scope of the vast and varied landscape without driving. San Francisco is a town for walking, with buses and cable-cars to help you up and down the hills, but Los Angeles is resolutely a drivers' town. Yosemite and Sequoia are wonderful places for hiking.

San Francisco (*CALIFORNIA*)

San Franciscans are unashamedly in love with their life. All over the place you see the boast: 'Everybody's Favorite City.' The town's natural setting, the hills around the bay, make it uncommonly cozy; the zip in the air is invigorating, and even the fog rolling off the ocean is romantic rather than chilling, the mists rolling over Twin Peaks, enveloping the Golden Gate Bridge or blanketing Golden Gate Park are sights not to be missed. The enthusiasm of the residents is difficult to resist, and easy to understand.

If you have a car, the best way to begin is by taking the **49-Mile Scenic Drive**, an 80km comprehensive tour that gives an overall picture before you explore in detail. Stop off at **Twin Peaks**, south of Golden Gate Park, for a panoramic view of the city and its bay. Then put away the car and use the city's first-class public transportation, combined with a pair of good walking shoes. The city is great to explore on foot, but be warned: the hills are every bit as steep as they look.

Start at the bridge. There is more than one, but *the* bridge is of course the **Golden Gate Bridge**. Named 'Golden Gate' for the channel it crosses, between San Francisco and Marin County, the bridge itself is colored a deep burned sienna or reddish-brown, depending on the light. At 4,200ft (1,280m), this masterpiece by engineer Joseph Strauss is not the longest, but many agree that it's the most

Distinctive city

San Francisco is a city of at least a dozen neighborhoods, each as distinct and original as the people who live in them.

The Golden Gate Bridge connects the city with Marin County

beautiful suspension bridge in the world. Completed in 1937, it took four years to build and takes four years to repaint – a job that begins again as soon as it's finished. Walking among the joggers and cyclists over the swaying bridge with its rattling lampposts is as exciting an adventure as climbing the Eiffel Tower in Paris.

While you're here, spare a thought for Oakland Bay Bridge, more commonly referred to as the **Bay Bridge** just visible in the distance. The silvery bridge swings across to Berkeley and Oakland, and at 8¼ miles (13.5km) is one of the world's longest.

Take in a magnificent view of the Golden Gate from Lincoln Park at 34th Avenue and Clement, the site of the **California Palace of the Legion of Honor** (tel: 415-750-3600; www. famsf.org), which was built as a memorial to the state's World War I casualties. A replica of the Legion of Honor Palace in Paris, the neoclassical building is now an art museum, housing collections of ancient art, European decorative art, painting, sculpture, and works on paper. A fine collection of Rodin's sculptures can be

Save your legs and take the cable-car

found here; at the entrance is one of the five existing bronze casts of his *The Thinker*.

On the way down to the Yacht Harbor is the **Palace of Fine Arts**, dating from the 1915 Panama-Pacific Exposition. The exterior, a hodge-podge of classical architecture and reinforced concrete evoking a Roman ruin, contrasts with the modern technological wizardry of the **Exploratorium** (3601 Lyon Street; tel: 415-563-7337; www.exploratorium.edu) inside. The museum's holography, lasers, and solar-operated musical instruments are great for the kids on a rainy day.

From the western Yacht Harbor make your way along Marina Boulevard, past pretty waterfront houses, to busy and bustling **Fisherman's Wharf**. Stroll around, look at the boats, and nibble shrimp or crab from the seafood stands along the wharf. Check out the stores and restaurants of **Ghirardelli Square**, a converted red-brick chocolate factory, and **The Cannery**, once a fruit-processing plant. Directly east of Fisherman's Wharf is the popular **Pier 39**, another complex of shops, restaurants, and entertainments. Visitors are rewarded with spectacular views of the bay, Alcatraz, and the Golden Gate Bridge.

The Hills: There are 40 hills, and they are San Francisco's pride. A tour of Nob Hill (Powell or California Street cable-car), Telegraph Hill (bus), and Russian Hill (cable-car) will give you a good sense of the past and present splendors of San Francisco's wealthy residents.

The imposing Victorian houses of **Nob Hill**, where the 'nobs,' or nabobs, lived, were wiped out in the 1906 earthquake – with one notable exception: the impressive brownstone house of James Flood, now the highly exclusive Pacific Union Club. You can't get in, but you can loiter (with appropriate decorum) in the hill's two landmark hotels – the Fairmont and the Mark Hopkins. The Mark Hopkins has a panoramic bar; the stiff price of a drink is worth it for the view, especially at sunset, and the bartenders do know how to shake a cocktail.

One of the best reasons for climbing **Telegraph Hill** is to reach the breathtaking view from the top of **Coit Tower**. Built with a bequest from a local widow in 1934 to honor the city's fire department, it is designed to recall the nozzle of a fire hose.

Russian Hill may be less opulent than the other two hills, but its gardens and immaculate little cottages are very appealing. Its name comes from the Russian enclave that made its home here. The constant ups and downs of the city's streets reach a crazy climax on **Lombard Street**, between Hyde and Leavenworth. After you negotiate the incredibly serpentine plunge, weaving in

Cable Capers

A delightful way of riding San Francisco's hills is aboard the fabled cable-cars. It's the most enjoyable transportation in town, as views pass by in slow, bumpy motion. Riding at night is particularly romantic. The lines are shorter, and the nocturnal ambience is delightful. Cars run until 10pm.

The cars were first installed in 1873, and one of the originals is in the Cable-Car Museum, which is also the system's working center, at Washington and Mason streets. The handmade cars are constantly refurbished and overhauled, so don't be surprised if a line is not in service. Riders are not allowed on with ice cream, because the boneshaking ride would likely land it in the lap of a fellow passenger.

Lombard Street with Telegraph Hill beyond

and out of the seven sudden bends, you won't quibble about its claim to be the 'crookedest street in the world.'

North Beach: In spite of its name, North Beach has no beach at all. It's the district north of the Broadway and Columbus intersection that is both center of the Italian community and focus of the city's artistic and intellectual life, centered around its many coffeehouses, cafés, and bistros. Part of North Beach used to be known as the 'Barbary Coast,' an infamous den of iniquity where sailors came for the brothels, while their captains shanghaied drunken or otherwise unconscious civilians for their crews.

Since the 1950s, when poet Lawrence Ferlinghetti gathered his fellow beatniks around his **City Lights Bookstore**, North Beach has been the place where San Francisco's new ideas, intellectual and other, are first tried out. The more literate of the hippies in the 1960s congregated here rather than the more hedonistic enclaves of Haight-Ashbury. In the 1970s it was the turn of the 'mellows,' the smiling younger brothers and sisters of the hippies, gliding around on quiet roller-skates, eating frozen yogurt, and espousing the newly emerging ecological causes.

Chinese newcomers are making inroads into the Asian and Italian neighborhood, clustered around Columbus, Stockton, Vallejo, and Green streets. But the seedy tradition of the Barbary Coast lives on in the (shrinking) number of topless joints on Broadway.

Chinatown: This expansive neighborhood has evolved from a ghetto imposed on the Chinese in the 19th century by the founders of the city into a proud, self-assertive community. Gone are the days of the Tong wars to establish control of the community's underworld and opium dens. The vicarious thrill that these adventures provided has been replaced by a general civic pride, although Chinatown's elders are now begining to show some concern for the future. Rising rents have been driving out family businesses, and the upwardly mobile have continued their exodus to the suburbs. More than 100,000 Chinese live in San Francisco, making it the largest Chinese community outside Asia. The week-long Chinese New Year celebrations in February are a major event in the city.

The main neighborhood is bounded by Broadway, Bush, Kearny, and Stockton, with eight blocks of Grant Avenue as its axis. An ornamental arch at the Bush Street end marks the south entry to Chinatown. Flanking it are two houses of Chinese design. The **Golden Gate Fortune Cookie Factory** on Ross Alley is particularly fun to visit.

On a smaller scale is **Japan Town** – J-Town to San Franciscans. Its Cultural and Trade Center at Geary between Laguna and Fillmore streets includes schools of cookery and

North Beach and the Transamerica Pyramid

Japanese flower arrangement, a Japanese theater, and a hotel with Japanese amenities – sunken baths, mattresses on tatami mats, kimonoed maids, and indoor rock gardens.

Civic Center: In the wedge formed by Market Street, the city's main thoroughfare, and Van Ness Street, is a sprawling complex of municipal, state, and federal buildings, recently cleaned and refurbished, and known collectively as Civic Center.

It was initiated in an ambitious burst of city planning after the 1906 earthquake, and the early structures are in Renaissance style. As well as **City Hall** and the Main Public Library, the complex includes the Veterans' Building, the War Memorial Opera House, where the United Nations Charter was first signed in 1945, and Symphony Hall. The **Asian Art Museum** (tel: 415-581-3500; www.asianart.org) houses one of the largest collections of Asian art in world, including a Chinese Buddha dating from AD336.

Union Square: For a shopping detour, go down Market Street and turn off at Powell. Union Square is the place to go for fashionable boutiques, specialty stores, flower stands, and large department stores. At the end of Market Street is the city's old ferry terminal. Meticulously restored and raptuously received, it is now **Ferry Building Marketplace**, an indoor food hall open seven days a weeks, with a farmers' market outside twice a week. Continue on to Montgomery Street, the heart of San Francisco's wealthy Financial District. You're not likely to miss the **Transamerica Pyramid**, an 853ft (260m) spike at the corner of Montgomery and Washington streets.

City Hall, part of Civic Center

SoMa: For a cultural detour, head across Market Street to the area called SoMa (**So**uth of **Ma**rket). **Yerba Buena Gardens** is an arts and entertainment complex interspersed with tranquil patches of greenery that occupies the entire block between 3rd and 4th streets. The complex overlooks the **Esplanade**, a pretty Downtown park. Adjacent to the Esplanade is a four-story entertainment complex sponsored by Sony, the **Metreon**, where big-screen movie theaters and technology feature prominently. International touring shows tend to roost at the **Center for the Arts**, where there are art shows, dances, and other events. **Mission Street** might

SoMa's got the MoMA – and the Yerba Buena Gardens, too

be the city's most cultural thoroughfare, with five museums as its periphery: the **Museum of the African Diaspora**; the **California Historical Society**; the architecturally interesting **Contemporary Jewish Museum**; the **Museum of Craft and Folk Art**; and the **Cartoon Art Museum**. Despite these starry neighbors, SoMa's biggest attraction is the **San Francisco Museum of Modern Art** (MoMA; 151 3rd Street; tel: 415-357-4000; www.sfmoma.org), with its collection of 15,000 works, including those by Max Ernst, Picasso and Paul Klee. Designed by Swiss architect Mario Botta, many think the building overshadows the collections inside, but the museum is still worth a visit if only to admire the sunlight effects in the entrance hall beneath the five-story glass-roofed staircase. Be sure to leave time to visit the museum's gift shop.

Golden Gate Park: Away from the skyscrapers of Downtown, take the No. 5 Fulton bus to get to Golden Gate Park. Originally nothing but sand dunes, the area was turned into its present lush parkland quite by chance – or so the story goes – when 19th-century urban planner John McLaren accidentally dropped the oats from his horse's nosebag and they sprouted. McLaren carried on from there and today San Franciscans have a delightful landscape of small lakes and hills, an arboretum, botanical gardens, playing fields, stables, and a popular open-air chess hangout. At the eastern end of the park there's a wonderful children's playground, and beyond it lies the **Haight-Ashbury** district of the 1960s 'flower children.' Although increasingly gentrified with a regular infusion of stores and boutiques, Haight-Ashbury continues to draw tourists reliving 1967's 'Summer of Love.'

Golden Gate Park includes two major museums clustered around the Music Concourse. The **de Young Museum** (tel: 415-750-3600; www.famsf.org), which houses a fine collection of American paintings, recently reopened in a new building with a bold, monolithic design. Not to be outdone, the **California Academy of Sciences** (tel: 415-321-8000; www.calacademy.org), which houses a natural history museum, an aquarium, and a planetarium, unveiled its new 'earthhouse' for an indoor rainforest. This is a groundbreaking, four-story sphere topped by a living, planted roof, the work of noted architect Renzo Piano. After visiting these two temples to modern design, you might like to stop in the park's lovely Japanese Tea Garden.

Alcatraz: Of all the cruise-tours available on San Francisco Bay, the most interesting is to the disused prison of Alcatraz (tel: 415-561-4926; www.nps.gov/alcatraz). On the island, park rangers conduct informative tours of the former home of Al Capone and other convicts too dangerous for normal prisons. There are also excellent, award-winning audio guides, giving recorded reminiscences from guards and prisoners. Alcatraz – the name comes from the Spanish *Isla de los Alcotraces* (Isle of Pelicans) – is a 12-acre

Alcatraz, sometimes referred to as 'the rock'

(5-hectare) rock with no arable soil. The water for the shrubs and trees growing today had to be brought in by the US Army, for whom it was a disciplinary barracks until 1934. A chilling 1½ miles (2.5km) of ice-cold treacherous currents, sharks, and raw sewage separate Alcatraz from the San Francisco shore. (Be sure to bring a sweater as the air in the bay is nippy, even in summer.) This was the ideal location for America's most notorious federal civil penitentiary, but enormously expensive in upkeep. In 1962, with each inmate costing $40,000 a year, Alcatraz was finally closed down.

Excursions from San Francisco

The Bay Area: Immediately north of San Francisco, at the southern tip of of Marin County, are the two charming little harbor towns of **Sausalito** and **Tiburon**, which you can reach either by car across the Golden Gate Bridge or by ferry. Tiburon is the quieter of the two, although both towns have a colorful Mediterranean atmosphere. Nearby you can see California's legendary Giant redwood trees close up at **Muir Woods National**

Giant redwoods at Muir Woods National Monument

Monument. Some of the trees here are 1,000 years old and grow to heights of 250ft (75m).

Wine Country: Wine-lovers will enjoy a drive through the vineyards of **Napa Valley** and across the Mayacama Mountains to **Sonoma Valley**. Napa, less than 50 miles (81km) northeast of San Francisco, lies between the Mayacamas and the Howell Mountains, stretching from the town of Napa in the south to Calistoga in the north. Highway 29 is the main route through the valley. The **Silverado Trail**, which runs parallel to it, is the slower, quieter, and more scenic route. The wineries provide tours and tastings in the cellars and organize picnics in the vineyards. Some of the larger wineries are at Sterling, and at Mondavi, Martini, Beaulieu, and Beringer in Napa, and at Souverain and Sebastiani in Sonoma Valley. Homesick French wine-lovers may want to visit the Domaine Chandon in Napa, owned by Chandon of Moët et Chandon fame. The smaller, family-run 'boutique' wineries offer distinctive wines, with tastings in relaxed and informal showrooms. The Napa Valley Conference and Visitors' Bureau (1310 Town Center Napa; tel: 707-226-7459; www.napavalley.com) can help with maps and information. The best restaurants of the region tend to be closed on Tuesdays.

Pacific Coast: Take Highway 101 south from San Francisco and join Pacific Highway, Route 1, at Castroville, to get to **Monterey**, the old Spanish and Mexican capital of Alta (Upper) California. The bay was discovered in 1542 but was not settled until 1770, when Father Junípero Serra set up a mission here with the garrison protection of Gaspar de Portola's *presidio*. Monterey was a bleak, disease-ridden place, and Portola recommended it be handed over to the Russians, who also coveted it, 'as a punishment.' But Father Serra accepted the hardships and led the taming of the Monterey wilderness. His statue keeps watch on Corporal Ewin Road.

The town offers a signposted tour of the Old Town's historic buildings from the 19th-century Mexican administration and early American period. The architecture mixes Spanish adobe and American colonial clapboard, two stories with a balcony – a hybrid which earns it the name of 'Monterey style.' At the Monterey Chamber of Commerce (380 Alvarado Street; tel: 831-648-5360; www.mpcc.com) you can get a map showing the major houses.

Look for the **Larkin House** at Jefferson and Calle Principal, home of the first (and only) US Consul, in the 1840s, and the **Robert Louis Stevenson House**, 530 Houston Street, where the writer lived while he was working on *Treasure Island*. On Church Street you'll find the site of Father Serra's original baked-mud church; rebuilt in 1795, it is now the **Royal Presidio Chapel** or Cathedral of San Carlos de Borromeo. To the left of the altar is an 18th-century *Virgin Mary* from Spanish Mexico.

Nearer the waterfront are the **Pacific House**, on Custom House Plaza, with a pleasant, flowery, and tree-shaded arcaded courtyard, and the **Custom House** (1827), taken over as the first US federal building on the Pacific Coast.

More distinctively American is **California's First Theater** on Scott and Pacific streets, a pinewood shack built by one Jack Swan in 1847 as a saloon with a dubious boarding house upstairs. Customers were (and still are) attracted by Victorian melodramas, but the 'boarding house' no longer operates.

Fisherman's Wharf, like San Francisco's attraction of the same name, is a collection of stores and restaurants out on the dock, but with a closer view of the boats. The fish here are almost always fresh, but not enough to keep **Cannery Row** as more than a weather-beaten curiosity. The fisheries along the row were the sardine capital of the western hemisphere from 1921 to 1946, but by 1951 the sardines had disappeared. Today, the timbered canneries made famous by novelist John Steinbeck are restaurants, boutiques, and art galleries.

A big draw is the **Monterey Bay Aquarium** (tel: 831-648-4800; www.mbayaq.org), featuring the denizens of the bay. With a wonderful Outer Bay exhibit holding 1 million gallons (4.5 million liters) of water, this spectacular aquarium furnishes viewers inside and out with the likes of barracuda, leopard sharks, anchovies, and delicately lovely jellyfish. At feeding time, divers don wetsuits and microphones to talk to spectators while underwater.

Farther on, the scenic **17-Mile Drive** (27.5km) winds through the Monterey Peninsula (fee; motorcycles not allowed), but you can also drive south directly to **Carmel**, a delightful resort and former artists' colony ideal for a rest and serious shopping. Just out

The spectacular cliffs of California's Highway 1

of town is the entrance to **Point Lobos State Park**, a compact gem of statuesque wind-blown rocks, pocket beaches and dramatic cliffs. Southeast of the town is the restored **Carmel Mission**, Basílica San Carlos Borromeo de Carmelo, where

Perfect timing

There are several types of tours to San Simeon. Lines can be long, but tickets are timed, so you can leave and come back again to enter almost immediately.

Father Serra is buried. The coast road from Carmel to Big Sur is only 30 miles (48km) long, but it takes over an hour of careful driving, and every hairpin turn reveals another spectacular vista.

Big Sur and the Pfeiffer–Big Sur State Park offer marvellous opportunities for picnics, camping, hiking, and fishing in the Big Sur River. The home of writer Henry Miller and other artists, Big Sur is a great place to escape the crowds.

The rugged shoreline road winds south for 65 miles (105km) more to where William Randolph Hearst, the man Orson Welles immortalized in *Citizen Kane*, built his dream home at San Simeon, now commonly referred to as **Hearst Castle** (guided tours, reservations advisable; tel: 800-444-4445; www.hearstcastle.org). Hearst himself called the 123 acres (50 hectares) of castle, guesthouse *palazzi*, terraces, gardens, Roman baths, private zoo, and tennis courts 'the Ranch.' Building began in 1919 and had still not been completed when the tycoon died in 1951.

The 275,000-acre (110,000-hectare) estate lies 1,600ft (500m) up in the hills. After parking in the lot, you take a tour bus which drives past zebras, barbary sheep, and goats grazing on the slopes – remnants of Hearst's private zoo.

San Francisco architect Julia Morgan built 'the Ranch' to Hearst's specifications as a 'functional showcase' for his art collection. The range of the collection registers as you pass the 100ft (30m) swimming pool with its Greek colonnade and a copy of Donatello's Florentine statue of *David* on two 17th-century baroque Venetian fountains. Over the gigantic main entrance, in quiet simplicity, is a (genuine) 13th-century *Madonna and Child*.

Los Angeles and Disneyland *(CALIFORNIA)*

LA's residents believe it's more a state of mind than a city. A state of mind covering 460 sq. miles (1,191 sq. km), bounded by sand and sea to the west, mountains to the north and east, and desert to the southeast, all with almost permanent sunshine. It's no surprise that leisure and pleasure are worshipped with little restraint here.

The Beach: The beach (Angelenos always refer to it in the singular) stretches some 40 miles (65km) from Malibu south through Santa Monica, Venice, Marina del Rey, Hermosa, and Redondo to Palos Verdes before the sands hit the pollution of Los Angeles Harbor and the Long Beach shipyards. There's no better way to get the special feel of Los Angeles than to go straight there. In LA, beaches are not just resorts for holidays and weekend cottages, they are year-round residential areas.

Looking out across LA

Malibu is home to the more relaxed members of the film community. The town sits in the 30-by-5-mile (48-by-8km) Santa Monica Mountains National Recreation Area, a network of federal, state, and county parks with nature trails overlooking fabulous beaches. Malibu Lagoon's Surfrider Beach attracts surfers worldwide, while Las Tunas and Topanga beaches are a little more peaceful. Malibu Pier is a good place to fish.

Built on more solid ground, **Santa Monica**'s beaches can be a family affair. The town's low-key, beach-resort vibes mask a sophistication that appeals to creative types, both Angelenos and out-of-towners, while leaving neighboring **Venice** to attract all the attention. The beach and beach park here are a non-stop open-air amateur circus of freaks, acrobats, weightlifters, clowns, and jugglers. In 1892, millionaire Albert Kinney wanted to create on the Pacific Coast a replica of Italy's Venice, complete

Joggers at Venice Beach

with canals, gondolas, a *palazzo* or two, hotels, and amusement arcades. Then somebody discovered oil and the idea was abandoned. Four canals remain with a Lighthouse Bridge that traverses the lagoon area feeding the canals. The neighborhood has revived as a community of artists, galleries, movie folk, and the ever-present bohemian types.

Hollywood: London buries its heroes in Westminster Abbey, Paris puts its great to rest in the Pantheon, and Los Angeles offers the hand, foot, and hoof prints of its stars in the cement courtyard of the fabulous **Grauman's Chinese Theatre** (6925 Hollywood Boulevard). So it's not a bad plan to start a Hollywood pilgrimage here. Sid Grauman had the idea in 1927 of getting the immortals' prints when they attended premieres at his exotic cinema. Most followed the example of the Marx Brothers and Rita Hayworth: they got on their knees and made a handprint. But it was natural for Fred Astaire to leave a footprint, and cowboy Tom Mix preferred leaving the hoof print of his horse.

Adjoining Grauman's is the **Kodak Theatre** (tel: 323-308-6300; www.kodaktheatre.com), home of the Oscars and part of the **Hollywood & Highland** complex. Tours can be taken where

The Strip

backstage guides provide the low-down on the gossip and the glitz. They take place daily from 10.30am–2.30pm (until 4pm in summer) and last half an hour.

Walk along **Hollywood Boulevard** (this is one part of LA where walking is customary) and you'll see over 2,500 actors' names on bronze stars embedded in the pavement – the famous **Walk of Fame**. Just steps away, in the beautiful old Art Deco Max Factor building, is the **Hollywood Museum** (tel: 323-464-7776; www.thehollywoodmuseum.com). On several levels in this fascinating place are costumes and location sets that most movie fans will recognize instantly, including the outrageous sets from *Moulin Rouge*, and in the basement, the spine-tingling cell that housed Hannibal Lecter in *The Silence of the Lambs*.

Back on the boulevard, you'll pass the beautifully restored **Roosevelt Hotel**, the site of the first public Oscars ceremony, and now a hip, happening place in its own right. North of the boulevard is the **Hollywood Bowl** (2301 North Hollywood Avenue; tel 323-850-2000; www.hollywoodbowl.com), the wonderful open-air auditorium where the Los Angeles Philharmonic Orchestra holds concerts against a background of the gigantic illuminated letters of the **H-O-L-L-Y-W-O-O-D sign** planted up in the hills. Across the street from the entrance is a barn that serves the small **Hollywood Heritage Museum**.

South of Hollywood Boulevard is **Sunset Boulevard**, the Hollywood section of which is known simply as '**the Strip**.' Once sleazy, the Strip is now the haunt of clubs and restaurants that attract the famous and glamorous. The Strip is the entrance to sassy, classy **West Hollywood**, which offers more of the same.

Downtown LA: When it was first built in 1928, **City Hall** (200 North Spring Street) was the tallest building in the city until height restrictions were lifted in 1957. An observation deck is open weekdays from 10am till 4pm. A few blocks northwest is the marble-and-glass **Music Center** (135 North Grand Avenue, tel: 213-972-7211; www.musiccenter.org), LA's cultural complex. As well as housing two theaters, the Music Center is the site of the **Walt Disney Concert Hall** (tel: 213-972-7282; www.laphil.com), home of the LA Philharmonic and designed by noted architect Frank Gehry in an explosion of metallic curves. Near Olvera Street and fabulous, still-in-use Art Deco **Union Station**, are some of the city's oldest buildings in a block-long stretch known collectively as **El Pueblo de Los Angeles Historic Monument** (tel: 213-628-1274; www.elpueblo.lacity.org). This includes the **Avila Adobe** LA's oldest, built in 1818.

Downtown's landmark buildings

The historic theater district on Broadway has evolved into a bustling Hispanic shopping street, well supplied with electronic goods and bridal gowns. A remnant of the proud theatrical past is the **Million Dollar Theater** (307 South Broadway), decorated with whimsical terracotta. The **Mayan Theater** (11th and Hill Street) is now a nightspot. From a terminal located on Fourth and Hill streets, the **Angels Flight** inclined railway carried Downtowners up and down Bunker Hill. Opened in 1901 as the 'Los Angeles Incline Railway,' the funicular

Downtown Los Angeles

0 ____ 500 yds
0 ____ 500 m

← Chinatown
← Hollywood
← Pasadena

Union Station
Olvera St
Avila Adobe
El Pueblo de Los Angeles Historic Monument
EL PUEBLO DE LOS ANGELES HISTORIC PARK
Cathedral of Our Lady of the Angels
Former Hall of Justice
US Ctr
Los Angeles Mall
Federal Building
MOCA at the Geffen Contemporary
Japanese American National Museum
E. 1st St
E. 2nd St
E. 4th St
North Alameda
South Alameda
Japanese Village Plaza
LITTLE TOKYO
New Otani Hotel
Japanese American Cultural & Community Center
S. Central Av
Crocker Towne
E. Temple St
City Hall
Parker Ctr
San Pedro St
East 3rd St
Los Angeles St
Hall of Administration
Music Center
Dorothy Chandler Pavilion
Walt Disney Concert Hall
Civic Center
County Ct
County Courthouse
Law Lib.
LA Times Building
Museum of Contemporary Art
California Plaza
Angels Flight
Grand Central Market
Bradbury Building
Wells Fargo History Mus.
US Bank Tower
Bunker Hill Steps
Pershing Square
Los Angeles World Trade Ctr
Union Bank Square
Westin Bonaventure Hotel
Central Library
Millennium Biltmore Hotel
Oviatt Building
Los Angeles Theatre
East 4th St
East 5th St
Winston
Wall St
Maple Av
S. Los Angeles St
East 6th St
East 7th St
S. Main St
South Main St
S. Spring St
S. Hill St
S. Olive St
S. Hope St
S. Flower St
S. Grand Av
South Grand Av
South Olive St
South Hill St
South Spring St
City National Plaza
Fine Arts Building
7th Street/Metro Ctr
Seventh Market Place
777 Tower
Museum of Neon Art
Original Pantry
Mayan Theater
Staples Center
Convention Center
West 1st St
West 3rd St
West 4th St
West 5th St
West 6th St
West 7th St
West Olympic
Beaudry Av
Boylston St
Maryland St
Lucas Av
Beacon St
Shatto St
Wilshire
Garland Av
Harbor Hwy
West Center Studios
LA West Center Studios
Bixel St
Ingraham St
Bixel St
11th St
Harbor Fwy (110)
Terminal Island →
West Olympic Blvd

N

Music Center
Civic Center
Broadway
Spring St
Main St
Hill St
Olive St
Grand Av
Flower St
Figueroa St
N. Figueroa St

(101)
(110)

has been restored but had to close following an accident in 2001. It has been due to 'reopen soon' ever since.

Not far away, the **Museum of Contemporary Art** (MoCA; 250 South Grand Avenue; tel: 213-621-1745; www.moca.org) is an impressive and massive gallery (one of three MoCA museums) that contains art created since the 1930s. The colorful Mexican life of the city can be sampled at **Grand Central Market**, north of Pershing Square. (The other great food market is the Farmers' Market, west of Beverly Hills at Fairfax and Third.)

Straight down Figueroa Street is another neighborhood, dominated by the Los Angeles Convention Center and **Staples Center**, a sports complex and home to LA's beloved Lakers basketball team, with its legion of movie-star fans. A $4.2 billion sports and entertainment district known as **LA Live** (www.lalive.com) has been opening, year by year, new businesses, theaters, and hotels.

The first phase was completed in 2007 when the **Nokia Theater** opened as a concert and awards show venue, but the attraction that will probably pull in the most visitors is the **Grammy Museum** (www.grammymuseum.org), with music exhibits spread across four floors of the center.

West of Downtown is another great thoroughfare, **Wilshire Boulevard**, which has become a living museum of the city's Art Deco architecture from the 1920s and 30s.

Beverly Hills: Exclusive and assertive, Beverly Hills' streets are lined with Rolls-Royces and Mercedes, the architecture of the mansions a money-mad mixture of Spanish, Gothic, Bauhaus, and Renaissance.

The town is very clean; littering is almost a capital crime. It's policed with formidable efficiency and, except for in the great shopping streets such as **Rodeo Drive**, walking is viewed with suspicion, especially at night. If you do want to take a walk here, it's a good idea to put on tennis or jogging clothes; the police will assume you're doing athletics. Only burglars, it seems, walk around Beverly Hills in 'normal' clothes.

Universal Studios

Universal Studios (Lankershim Boulevard, north of the Hollywood Freeway; www.universalstudios.com): offers an elaborate tour in open trolleys with guides who have all the showbiz flair of Hollywood itself. Participating in the special-effects trickery, you'll be attacked by spaceships and the shark from *Jaws*, you'll meet a three-story King Kong, and experience all the earthquakes, flash floods, and fires you ever saw in disaster movies. You'll visit sound stages and back lots and learn the screen techniques used to create film's great illusions. You'll see how Moses parted the waters of the Red Sea in *The Ten Commandments* and ride through a 'town' that includes a New England fishing village, a Bavarian square, French bistros, and an Italian pizzeria, all in the space of four blocks.

Disneyland (Anaheim, 27 miles/44km southeast of Downtown LA on the Santa Ana Freeway; http://disneyland.disney.go.com): You might want to think about buying a one-, two-, or three-day passport that covers the whole Disneyland complex, which is good for unlimited use of the attractions.

Pick up a booklet with maps at City Hall and head down **Main Street**, which sets the tone with its sunny evocation of small-town USA. You may notice that all the houses and stores are three-quarter-size. In this effort to escape from the realities of the outside world, everything is a little smaller than life-size, and larger than life. Don't linger in the stores: head for **Fantasyland**, with Sleeping Beauty Castle, Pinocchio's Ride, and a boat cruise through the charming, disarming 'It's a Small World.'

Adventureland is a boat ride through simulated jungle foliage on a river that passes successively through Asia, Africa, and the South Pacific, complete with plastic tigers and alligators. A miniature railroad takes you through **Frontierland**, the pioneer country of the Old West, where a loudspeaker warns you to 'watch out for Indians and wild animals.' Just the faintest unease is aroused by a settler's cabin on fire with a wax-model pioneer lying outside, killed by an arrow. But at the end of each ride are reassuring ice-cream and soft-drink stands.

One of the most exciting themes is **Tomorrowland**, constantly being renovated to keep pace with progress. The rides include a submarine, the head-spinning Space Mountain, Star Tours, and some of the most up-to-date experiments in public transportation.

Disney's California Adventure: A separate theme park that traces the history and social culture of the Golden State with a series of thrill rides, cowboys, and themed 'lands.'

Downtown Disney: A monorail ride away, this is the shopping, eating, and nighttime district, with clubs and a cinema complex.

Museums in Los Angeles

The **LA County Museum of Art** (5905 Wilshire Boulevard; tel: 323-857-6000; www.lacma.org), designed by William Pereira, is one of the largest of its kind in the country. The permanent collections include Impressionist paintings, contemporary art, Indian and Islamic art, American art, and the Armand Hammer collection of Roman glass. In addition, the Pavilion for Japanese Art and the sculpture garden also contain some outstanding works, and there are regularly changing exhibitions of contemporary art.

The **Norton Simon Museum** in Pasadena (411 West Colorado Boulevard, off the Ventura Freeway; tel: 626-449-6840; www.nortonsimon.org) contains a collection of European paintings, drawings, and sculpture from the early Renaissance to the 20th

The Getty Center

century, plus Indian bronzes and Asian stone carvings.

The **Arm and Hammer Museum** (10899 Wilshire Boulevard; tel: 310-443-7000; www.hammer.ucla.edu), the legacy of yet another billionaire, contains the world's largest collection of Daumier's works, in addition to much other Western European art.

The **Getty Center** (1200 Getty Center Drive; tel: 310-440-7300; www.getty.edu) is LA's arts and cultural complex, perched on a 110-acre (44-hectare) site in the Santa Monica Mountains. Designed by architect Richard Meier, the sprawling campus includes the Getty Research Institute's 750,000-volume research library and houses the Getty Museum's permanent collection of paintings, illuminated manuscripts, and French decorative arts. The setting, the campus, and the view are worth the visit, although the collection is surprisingly modest. Admission is free, but an advance timed ticket is required. Fee for parking.

The **Getty Villa** (17985 Pacific Coast Highway; tel: 310-440-7300; www.getty.edu) is a museum in a lovely Malibu setting, dedicated to the study of ancient Greece, Rome, and Etruria.

San Diego (CALIFORNIA)

It was at San Diego that Portuguese captain Juan Rodríguez Cabrillo first set foot on California soil in 1542. Sixty years later, its bay was explored by the Spanish, but it wasn't until 1769 that Father Junípero Serra built his first mission.

The best way to appreciate San Diego's beauty is from the sea. Take a **cruise** along the bay – they start from Harbor Drive at the end of Broadway – past the manmade Harbor and Shelter islands around the tip of the peninsula to Point Loma out on the Pacific. Back on dry land, you can visit one of the 19th-century ships moored on the Embarcadero as part of the Maritime Museum Fleet, the most picturesque being the iron-hulled square rigger, *Star of India*, built in 1863. Or drop into Seaport Village, a lively complex of stores, restaurants, and galleries.

San Diego's discovery is celebrated by the **Cabrillo National Monument** on the Point Loma promontory (follow the signs southwest on Rosecrans Street). Cabrillo's statue, donated by the Portuguese government, faces the spot at which he landed.

Old Town (bounded by Juan, Twiggs, Congress, and Wallace streets) is a six-block area of restored adobe buildings from the city's Mexican era, plus the brick houses of early American settlers. You'll enjoy a rest under the palms and eucalyptus trees of Plaza Vieja, originally the center and bullring of the old pueblo. The **Gaslamp Quarter**, a mostly Victorian neighborhood Downtown, is another popular spot for strolling. Victorian architecture reaches its zenith on the nearby Coronado Peninsula, where the extravagant **Hotel del Coronado** (1888) has a distinguished guest list that has included everyone from John F. Kennedy to Britain's Prince of Wales.

The modern town is blessed with enlightened urban planning, the popular **Horton Plaza** shopping center, and the

Hotel del Coronado

Heading upcountry

wonderful **Balboa Park**. Set right in the center of town, the park offers a wealth of sports facilities and many of the city's excellent cultural attractions. There's even an Elizabethan playhouse, site of the summer Shakespeare festival.

The star of the park is the **San Diego Zoo** (2920 Zoo Drive; tel: 619-685-3200; www.sandiegozoo.com), acclaimed as one of the world's finest. Certainly it's one of the most progressive, giving the animals as large and natural a living space as possible in the confines of a manmade park. Australian species are particularly well represented. You can skim over the zoo in the Skyfari aerial tramway or take a guided bus tour.

Another great park is at **Mission Bay**, with first-class aquatic amenities. Paddle around tiny islands and lagoons in canoes, or sail in catamarans and full-size sloops. It is also the home of **Sea World** (tel: 619-226-390; www.seaworld.com), where you can see the famous 3-ton killer whale, as well as sea lions, otters, and a walrus.

California National Parks and Monuments

The best times of the year for Yosemite and Sequoia are spring and fall. Winter offers good cross-country skiing in Yosemite and lovely snowscapes in Sequoia, but check ahead to find out which roads are closed. Summer in both parks is crowded, but the peace of the high country is always within reach. Death Valley is best from late fall to early spring. In the height of summer, temperatures can rise to 100°F (37°C) or even higher.

Yosemite: One of the most breathtaking US national parks is Yosemite (www.nps.gov/yose). 'Base camp' – which might be a plush hotel room, modest lodge accommodations, or simply a tent – is at the heart of **Yosemite Valley** along the Merced River. From the valley you can hike, cycle (rentals at Yosemite Lodge or Curry Village), ride a horse or mule, or take the shuttle bus to all the sights. Soaring granite cliffs enclose the valleys: **Half Dome** at the northeast end (8,842ft/2,695m); Glacier Point, Sentinel, and Cathedral Spires down the south wall; and **El Capitan**, Three Brothers, and Washington Column up the north wall.

You can grade the hikes according to your capacity and endurance. In the Merced River Canyon, **Vernal Falls** is within the scope of any normally healthy person. A well-marked path begins at Happy Isles Nature Center, where knowledgeable park rangers will answer your questions. If you're up to it, push on along the Mist Trail, past Emerald Pool to **Nevada Falls**, and you'll begin to lose the crowd. Here you're on the John Muir Trail, named after the Scottish naturalist who explored the Sierra Nevada Mountains and made their conservation against the encroachments of civilization his life's work. The trail passes Merced Lake to the lovely **Tuolumne Meadows** in the high country. The final destination is Mt Whitney, over 200 miles (320km) away.

El Capitan, Yosemite

Less exhausting is a drive or shuttle-bus ride past Badger Pass to **Glacier Point**, 7,214ft (2,199m) above sea level. Both the altitude and the view over the whole valley and the High Sierras beyond are breathtaking. You can see Yosemite Creek drop half a mile (0.8km) from the opposite wall in two spectacular plunges (Upper and Lower **Yosemite Falls**) and also get an outstanding view of majestic Half Dome. From here you can hike and picnic on your way back along the Panorama Trail via the Nevada and Vernal falls – 8 miles (13km) downhill in all.

Another beautiful hike is out to **Mirror Lake**, especially in spring or early summer when the waters are perfectly still in the early morning or at sunset, capturing the marvelous colors from the trees and Mt Watkins behind.

Sequoia and Kings Canyon: This joint national park (www.nps. gov/seki) is a haven of peace and contemplation among the giant sequoias, the largest living creations on earth, many of them nearly 3,000 years old. The forest offers a gorgeous array of dog-woods, sugar pines, and white firs, and a rich flora of orange leopard lily, white corn lily, lupine, chinquapin, and bracken fern. This is no place for a hurried look; walk slowly, sit quietly, and listen; fall asleep under a tree. Watch for the birds – woodpeck-er, raven, spotted owl, but also W.C. Field's favorite, the moun-tain chickadee, and the Steller's jay.

Start at the **Giant Forest Village** with its motel and the Park Rangers' Visitor Center at Lodgepole, where you can get a map and information about the best walks in the forest and hikes in the backcountry. The best introduction to the forest is the **Con-gress Trail**. It's an easy 2-mile (3km) walk that begins at the **General Sherman Tree**, the biggest of them all, 275ft (84m) high, 103ft (31m) around its base and still growing. Reaching up for the light well above the rest of the forest, the branches start 130ft (40m) above the ground. As you move among the other great sequoias – the President, the Senate Group, the House Group, and the General Lee – you can understand John Muir waxing lyrical about 'the first tree in the forest to feel the touch of rosy beams of morning and the last to bid the sun goodnight.' Another beautiful walk, by no means an exhausting hike, is out to **Crescent Meadow**, passing more of the stately giants along the way.

If you want to get away and explore the backcountry, carry on along the High Sierra Trail running 11 miles (18km) from Crescent Meadow to **Bearpaw Meadow**. This is not too formidable a hike. A nearby lake and streams offer good trout-fishing, and there's a fair chance of spotting some of the park's bobcats, coyotes, golden eagles, black bear, spotted skunk, and cougar.

Death Valley: A convenient way to see Death Valley (www. nps.gov/deva) is to combine it with a trip to Las Vegas. Come from the east, either on Highway 95 and via Death Valley Junction on Route 190, or farther north via Beatty, on Route 58.

This desert is perhaps the greatest surprise of all the wonders of California. It's not one but a dozen landscapes, not a monotonous expanse of sand dunes but an endless variety of terrains, rock formations, colors, and plants. Come here in winter and you may see

Death Valley

a flood of spring flowers blooming in the wake of the sparse rains. But above all, there's the light, uncannily clear, distorting distances, pink at dawn, white at mid-morning, piercing silver at noon, and then shimmering into gold as the afternoon progresses.

Don't be deterred by the name Death Valley. It was bequeathed by unlucky Gold Rush hopefuls who crossed from Arizona and Nevada and suffered bitter hardships here. There are now some excellent facilities at **Furnace Creek**. However, if you are crossing the desert in summer, do not drive off the main road and, if you break down, wait in your car for the next police patrol. Also take plenty of gasoline and drinking water.

Get up at dawn – really, you won't regret it – and drive out southeast along Highway 190 to **Zabriskie Point**. As the sun rises and the light hits Tucki Mountain and the tips of the Panamints to the west before plunging into the valley's primeval salt-lake bed below, you're likely to be set wondering about the world's creation. By mid-morning (if you visit in winter) the temperature could be something like a cool 50°F (10°C) on your exposed ridge, but walk down the hill to the lake bed and you'll feel the heat rising to meet you, reaching the 80s°F (20s°C) by the time you get to the bottom.

Continue over to **Dante's View** (altitude 5,745ft/1,751m), looking down at **Badwater**, 282ft (86m) below sea level, and the lowest point in the United States. Make up your own mind whether this is paradise, purgatory, or hell. On the other side of the valley are Wildrose, Bennett, and Telescope peaks.

Craps, a popular Las Vegas game

Las Vegas (NEVADA)

If European and American dreamers go to California, where do Californian dreamers go? Well, they take Interstate 15

The Fremont Street Experience

to Las Vegas, one of those myth-laden towns that everybody should visit at least once.

In Downtown Vegas, which has banks and professional buildings cheek to jowl with casinos, the neon lights are so bright that midnight can look like noon back in the Mojave. Focus for all the action is **Fremont Street**, or 'Glitter Gulch.' Every lit-up window shows dozens of people tugging the levers of the 'one-armed bandit' slot machines. One neon sign declares: 'For every US coin you got, we got the slot.'

Downtown is also the site of the spectacular **Fremont Street Experience** (www.vegasexperience.com; hourly after dark), an eye-popping computer-generated light spectacular that spans several city blocks. This free show is the best value in Vegas.

To all who visit, Las Vegas Boulevard is just known as **The Strip**, a solid 4 miles (6.5km) of hotels and casinos, each with neon wattage advertising America's top stage productions, comedians, and singers, and a score of girlie shows – on ice, in water, even on an ordinary stage. Although Las Vegas has stopped aggressively

Bellagio is one of the most lavish resorts in Vegas

marketing itself as a family destination, there's still wholesome entertainment around, too, including several theme parks.

An evening walk along The Strip offers more entertainment than most cities can provide in a week. These are the true monuments of Las Vegas; the re-creations in casino form of the Great Pyramid at **Luxor**; the Piazza San Marco and Grand Canal at **The Venetian**; and the scaled-down pastiche of the Manhattan skyline at **New York-New York**. There are palaces of the Orient, ancient Rome, Paris, and other places of exotic fable. **Bellagio** is an Italianate marvel, styled after the shoreline of Lake Como with its elegant fountains of dancing waters; **Caesars Palace** offers the decadent style of ancient Rome with Italian marble colonnades. But there's much, much more: the medieval **Excalibur**; the **Mirage**'s gardens, palm trees, and ever-erupting volcano, now bigger and better than ever; the manmade mountain and waterfalls of Vegas's most luxurious resort, **Wynn Las Vegas**. **T.I.** (Treasure Island) has a streetside sea battle featuring booming cannon fire, scantily clad females, and swashbuckling male pirates. Every hour.

All this extravaganza is here to provide an exhilarating backdrop to the gambling – hundreds of slot machines spill out from the casinos into the lobbies, plus roulette tables, baccarat, blackjack, and bingo. Poker is usually played in a roped-off area at sedate tables attended by house dealers too busy keeping the game going to crack a joke. The most enjoyable tables for spectators are the dice or craps games. Players get very excited as the 'bones' roll. They whoop, cheer and groan as their fortunes change. Two things that you won't see in the casinos are clocks or windows – the management doesn't want you distracted. As a result, the action is non-stop. Come to be amazed.

Seattle (WASHINGTON)

Bright and energetic, Seattle is blessed with one of those natural locations that render public relations unnecessary. Its bay on Puget Sound is surrounded by the green, green country of Washington state. The snow-capped Olympic and Cascade mountains loom in the background and 14,410ft (4,392m) Mt Rainier towers over them all. The climate is fresh and moist, hence the town's sobriquet of the Emerald City. In spring and summer the place positively sparkles.

Seattle's fortunes were very much tied to those of the Boeing aircraft manufacturers, as the lumber industry, which got the town started in the 1850s, began to decline. But Bill Gates's Microsoft, amazon.com and a whole host of other dot commers took the city to unprecedented prosperity. The deepwater Pacific harbor has made a natural gateway for trade with Asia, and the city benefits from a lively Chinatown as well as a Japanese community. It was also the springboard for the Alaska and Klondike gold rushes of the 1880s and 1890s.

Pacific wanderlust

It's easy to travel around the Pacific Northwest. From Seattle, you can take a train south to Portland, Oregon, or even on to San Francisco. Heading north, jump aboard an excursion boat to Victoria, in Canada.

Pioneer Square (First Avenue and Yeslerway) is the only vestige of those gold-rush days. Its Victorian red brick has been spared the urban developers' wrecking ball, and the pleasant tree-shaded little square is surrounded by good restaurants, boutiques, and a couple of excellent jazz clubs.

You can explore Seattle's lower depths on an **Underground Tour** (from 608 First Avenue; tel: 206-682-4646; www.underground tour.com). It leads through the subterranean city that was burned out in 1889 and buried under today's buildings, which were simply erected on top. You'll see old stores and facades and eerie galleries, illuminated by the guide's amusing stories.

Like any self-respecting port, Seattle is liveliest along the **waterfront**. Seafood restaurants, fish stands, and chandlers share the area along Elliott Bay with parks and the **Seattle Aquarium** (Pier 59; tel: 206-386-4300; www.seattleaquarium. org). Stop by to feast your eyes on octopuses, sharks, eels, seals, and salmon, or watch a film on the watery depths in the Omnidome theater. Afterwards, when it's time to get out on the water yourself, harbor tours and a variety of ferry rides will fit the bill.

The Olympic Sculpture Park and the Space Needle beyond

Also on the waterfront, the daily **Pike Place Market** (Pike Street and First Avenue) is where farmers, fishmongers, and butchers sell their own produce. It's delightful to see views of the water through huge piles of tomatoes or flowers. Farther north along the waterfront is one of the city's newer attractions, the **Olympic Sculpture Park**. This world-class outdoor permanent display is organized by the **Seattle Art Museum** (University and First Avenue; tel: 206-654-3100; www.seattle artmuseum.org), itself worth a visit. The **Seattle Asian Art Museum** in Volunteer Park is another branch of this museum. Stop in to marvel at Seattle's **Central Library** (4000 First Avenue; tel: 206-386-4636; www.spl.org): the 11-story exterior has a dazzling skin of

Pike Place Market

glass and steel, while the interior is better than many museums.

The **International District**, bounded by Fourth and Eighth avenues and Main and Lane streets, includes Chinatown and the Japanese neighborhood. You'll find lots of jade and jewelry stores here, as well as restaurants, a Buddhist temple, and the **Wing Luke Asian Museum** (719 South King Street; tel: 206-623-5124; www.wingluke.org), which calls itself 'the only pan-Asian Pacific American museum' in the United States.

The great symbol of Seattle is the 607ft (185m) **Space Needle** (tel: 206-905-2100; www.spaceneedle.com; open until midnight on weekends), standing on a tripod. This is a relic from the 1962 World's Fair. The revolving restaurant and observatory at the top give splendid views across the city to the Olympic Mountains and the Cascade Range dominated by Mt Rainier. Right below the Needle is the **Seattle Center** (tel: 206-684-7200; www.seattle center.com), which also grew out of the World's Fair. Its buildings consist of an opera house, a playhouse, the Coliseum, two theaters, a sculpture garden, three first-rate museums and much more. It also houses the **Pacific Science Center**, a good-looking structure with exhibits on space exploration, the Northwest Indian culture, and the oceanography of Puget Sound.

The fabulous **Experience Music Project** (tel: 206-770-2700; www.empsfm.org) is a state-of-the-art interactive museum celebrating the creative process in pop music. The amazing building, designed by Frank Gehry, is said to resemble the inside of a guitar. Fans of Jimi Hendrix (Hendrix was born near Seattle) should plan to spend at least a day here, while sci-fi fans will enjoy EMP's **Science Fiction Museum and Hall of Fame**.

If the silhouette of Mt Rainier (14,410ft/4,392m), an active volcano encased in miles of snow and ice, has proved too tempting to resist, why not take an excursion to **Mt Rainier National Park**? It's only two hours south of Seattle, and there are exhilarating hikes to be enjoyed.

Far West States

Alaska: This is the largest state in the USA, encompassing a vast area of infinite variety. A popular misconception is that it is all a frozen wasteland. The **Southeastern Panhandle**, from Ketchikan via Juneau up to Haines and Skagway, has a moderate climate, a lot of rain, and fertile land, with considerable forests. The **Gulf Coast**, north and west of Haines around the Gulf of Alaska, is the most densely populated, centering on **Anchorage**, the state's only real metropolis.

The **Western region**, including the Alaskan Peninsula and the Aleutian and Pribilof islands, is foggy, wet, and windy; great for sea- and bird-life. The **Interior** south of the Brooks Range from the Canadian Yukon border toward the Bering Sea has a dry climate and is warm in summer, bitterly cold in winter. And the Arctic, extending from Kotzebue above the Seward Peninsula in the west around Barrow to the North Slope at Prudhoe Bay, has a bleak landscape of permanently frozen soil.

A great way to see Alaska is by boat. Ships cruise from Seattle and (in summer) Vancouver, San Francisco, and Los Angeles.

Beach life in Hawaii

Hawaii: The 50th and newest state of the US is an archipelago of seven inhabited islands and a collection of islets, reefs, sandbars, and rocks strung out over 1,500 sq. miles (2,430 sq. km) in the North Pacific. The state's capital, Honolulu, is a modern high-rise city on the island of **Oahu**. The long white beaches and blue ocean are perfect for swimming and sunbathing; surfers swear by the waves on Oahu's North Shore. Waikiki offers the best nightlife.

The island of **Hawaii** is known locally as the 'Big Island' because of its size and to distinguish it from the state name. The main feature is the volcanoes, particularly the still-active Kilauea Crater. **Maui** has wonderful beaches and plenty of sports facilities, as well as the old royal capital of Lahaina. A visit to the 10,000ft (3,000m) dormant volcano Haleakala is a must.

Farther north, the islands of **Molokai** and **Lanai** are ideal for those who want a quiet vacation, with good opportunities for hiking, mule-trekking, and rugged trips by Jeep. **Kauai**, the Garden Island, is a lush tropical paradise, where the rivers and waterfalls are a delight for fishing enthusiasts.

WHAT TO DO

The diversity of America offers almost every kind of recreational activity: cultural, sporting, or artistic, and at a level as rarified or as popular as you could wish for. Outdoor landscapes of all kinds provide scope for climbing, swimming, hiking, and cycling. Although spectator sports are mostly American varieties – baseball, basketball, ice hockey, and American football – they all offer terrific entertainment value. Theaters and showrooms present everything from *Chicago* to the Ring Cycle to Bruce Springsteen.

SPORTS

Few countries are more sports-conscious than America. The competitive spirit runs high in every activity, and facilities are first-rate.

Watersports

The Atlantic coasts of New England, New York, New Jersey, the Carolinas, and Florida, and the Pacific Coast of California provide every imaginable kind of watersport – from swimming and diving to boating and fishing. There are stores at the seaside resorts where you can rent the necessary equipment for surfing, snorkeling, scuba-diving, windsurfing, and waterskiing. Inland towns like Chicago or Detroit provide similar facilities on their lakes and rivers.

Long-time reputations hold that southern California or Hawaii are best for **surfing**. On the West Coast, the best waves are on Point Duma in Malibu, Surfrider at Santa Monica State Beach, and at La Jolla on Windansea and Boomer. In Hawaii, go to the island of Oahu. Waikiki has the history and the waves, while Sunset Beach on the North Shore is for experts only.

For **sailing**, Long Island Sound (New York and Connecticut), Cape Cod (Massachusetts), Newport (Rhode Island), Chesapeake Bay

Grand Canyon river-runners wait for the rapids

Kayaking in the Everglades

(Maryland and Virginia), and Fort Lauderdale (Florida) are among the best on the East Coast, while Pacific sailors swear by San Diego (California) and Seattle (Washington).

Canoeing, a leisurely sport in the Florida Everglades, becomes an exhilarating test of endurance on the Colorado River in Arizona and Utah or in Yellowstone Park.

Deep-sea fishing provides high adventure in the waters off Florida, but is equally satisfying up around Cape Cod, along the Outer Banks of North Carolina, or off the northern California coast. Check with local information centers for **freshwater fishing** licensing regulations.

Outdoor Activities

There are marvelous opportunities for **hiking** all around the country, from the national parks of the west to the hills of New England. The famous Appalachian Trail that runs all the way from Maine down to Georgia is a great way to escape the crowds.

Wear good walking boots, not soft-soled shoes, for the longer hikes, and warm clothing is needed for the cool evenings in the mountains. The rangers who run the national parks can help you with maps and directions to the more interesting nature trails.

If you want to try **mountain climbing,** it's always best to go with an experienced guide, especially over unfamiliar terrain. You can rent equipment in the larger national parks; call the park rangers for information.

Hunting in the Rockies for moose and gamebirds is carefully regulated but by no means forbidden. Check with the local tourist information or park rangers for information about permits.

Jogging is still a popular pastime, and healthiest of all when done barefoot along a sandy beach. The town parks often have marked trails with exercise stations en route. In Boston, for instance, the parks, which locals call their 'emerald necklace' strung along both banks of the Charles River, are perfect for jogging. Alternatively, you can rent a **bicycle** or even a pair of **rollerblades**.

Tennis, **golf**, and **squash** are also popular. Tennis has grown to such an obsession that many towns provide floodlit public courts for nighttime matches. Frequently the larger hotels will have at least one tennis court on their grounds, and sometimes they can help you with access to the local golf clubs. It's a good idea to take your home golf-club membership card, but there are also many municipal golf courses open to the public.

Horseback riding is good in New England and California. In the country's national parks, it's one of the more satisfying ways to get off the beaten path.

If you're taking a winter vacation, **skiing**, both cross-country and downhill, is spectacular in Colorado, Utah, and California, but there are also good family resorts in New England. You may find the après-ski a little slow, but the slopes are fine and people tend to take turns at the ski lifts, rather than push to the front.

A round of golf in Arizona

Spectator Sports
Don't let the unfamiliarity of **American football** or **baseball** discourage you from watching these exciting games. An hour of the raucous humor of a base-ball crowd for the New York

Yankees or the Boston Red Sox, the militant religious fervor of football fans at a Dallas Cowboys game, or the stoical fatalism of Chicago Bears supporters will teach you more about the local community than any sociological monograph.

Other sports, such as **basketball** and **ice hockey**, are played out in a particularly electric atmosphere, charged up in basketball by a lot of gambling on the 'points spread' (points difference between the two teams). **Soccer** has gained a higher profile in recent years due to British sports hero and international pin-up David Beckham joining the ranks of the Los Angeles Galaxy.

Tennis is best witnessed at the US Open Championships at New York's Flushing Meadow in September. The only thing drowning out the roar of the jumbo jets flying over from La Guardia Airport is the clamor of the spectators. And yet the tension somehow brings out the best in the players.

An unusual sport played in Newport, Rhode Island, and in Florida is **jai alai** (pronounced 'high lie'), a local version of the high-

Football players in action

speed Basque game *pelota*. It's
played in a three-walled court,
trapping and hurling the ball
with a scooped reed-basket
known as a *cesta*. Night games
in Florida are played at the
Miami Jai Alai Fronton.

Horse racing attracts some
colorful characters to Aqueduct
and Belmont Park in New York
and to Santa Anita near Los
Angeles. But the great moment
of the racing year is in Louisville for the Kentucky Derby
(pronounced 'Der-bee') in May.
If you are in the country at the
time but can't get to Louisville,

Baseball – the field of dreams

you can still attend one of the countless Kentucky Derby parties
held around the country, often in neighborhood bars. Several hours
are spent drinking mint juleps (bourbon with crushed ice, sugar,
and fresh mint), but the race itself lasts just two minutes.

SHOPPING

The most important advice we can give you on shopping in the US
is not to start on your first day or you may find you'll have to go
home early. For Americans, the business of seducing the consumer
has become a fine art, and shopping is more or less the national
pastime. America is also the home of the 'outlet store,' and these
bargain bazaars can offer some retail therapy.

Outlet stores have become so established now that outside
most major towns and cities are outlet malls – clusters of discount sheds. The outlets provide end-of-line and last season's
fashion goods and famous-label designer gear. Polo Ralph
Lauren, Nike, Swatch, Gap, Liz Claiborne, and Banana Republic

Souvenirs of a New York stay

all make regular appearances in outlets and outlet malls and offer great savings for label queens of both sexes.

East Coast Shopping

Europeans find **New York** discount prices advantageous for cameras and electronics. In the realm of gadgets, Hammacher Schlemmer (147 East 57th Street) and The Sharper Image (4 West 57th) reign supreme. The best toy stores are F.A.O. Schwarz (Fifth Avenue and 58th Street), and the gigantic Toys R Us in Times Square.

Manhattan's department stores are an exciting world of their own. Bloomingdale's now has two branches; Barneys continues to innovate styles and trends, and then there's ever-popular Macy's, which bills itself as the world's largest store.

Boston's importance in the nation's history makes it an ideal place to find the best of old Americana, but it becomes increasingly difficult to get the authentic stuff without historic prices. In antiques shops in Charles Street on Beacon Hill or Harvard Square in Cambridge you'll find original, sturdy early furniture, but more often good reproductions. Patchwork quilts are another specialty of colonial days, as well as decorative lacy-patterned glassware and handmade pewter. Although whaling days are over, you can still find delicately carved scrimshaw made from whalebone and walrus tusks (particularly in curio shops in Back Bay or around Cape Cod and on Nantucket). Fragrant green candles made from bayberries are a specialty of Cape Cod.

Washington is a terrific museum town, and the museums also provide the best place to buy unusual and attractive gifts. The Air and Space Museum store has great model aircraft and spaceships for children and the young at heart. The Museum of Natural History has jewelry of semiprecious stones and beautifully mounted pieces of rare minerals. The main Smithsonian Bookstore, in the Museum of American History, offers a comprehensive selection of books on the country's arts, history, and technology. Near the Mall entrance, take time to browse through the museum store, which sells replicas of the more popular exhibits of old Americana.

The National Geographic Society (17th and M streets NW) is also well worth visiting for its wonderful maps and picture-books of places near and far. For posters of the great masters, art calendars, and art books, try the stores at the National Gallery of Art, both East and West, and the Hirshhorn Museum.

Macy's always pulls in the crowds

Study the newspapers, especially the Sunday editions, which are filled with advertising about the sales or 'specials' currently promoted in the big stores. The major cities have discount stores, particularly good for cameras, electronic equipment, and sporting goods. The press also gives details of local flea markets, generally held only on weekends.

West Coast Shopping

San Francisco is a fine place for shopping. Several small shopping centers, such as The Cannery, Pier 39, or Ghirardelli Square, are clustered around Fisherman's Wharf. These may specialize in tacky tourist junk, but among all the T-shirts are some out-of-the-ordinary souvenirs: colorful dragons to hang in the wind, unusual toys, bizarre sunglasses, or 'food art,' perfect for the next party.

One place to check out is Ghirardelli's Chocolate Shop. Now exported all over the United States, this yummy candy was first made in Ghirardelli Square in 1895. Most shopping is centered around Market Street and Union Square. Barneys, Bloomingdale's, Neiman-Marcus, Macy's, and Sak Fifth Avenue are all here, together with smaller retailers, jeans stores, and antiques shops. For great fashions and amusing bric-a-brac, try elegant Union Street.

Los Angeles glitters with conspicuous consumption, and few places shine as brightly as Rodeo Drive. Two complexes here draw in the beautiful and the wealthy: the Rodeo Collection, a pinkish mall on two levels specializing mostly in fashion, and the faux-cobbled winding street Two Rodeo Drive, home to Tiffany, Cartier, and Dior.

A mile (1.5km) to the east is Century City, where the shopping center and marketplace have stores, theaters, and restaurants whose

Garage Sales

A fine American institution for bargains in secondhand goods is the garage sale. Families moving away or just periodically emptying out their attics and cellars offer old clothes, furniture, books, records, and ornaments, displayed in the driveway of their garage. Track them down from handwritten advertisements posted on walls, lampposts, or supermarket notice boards, or by just driving slowly around residential neighborhoods on summer Saturdays – you're bound to find more than one. They're great places to discover a particular type of Americana – ashtrays, car license plates, tobacco tins – that Americans consider junk and Europeans consider collectibles.

validation will give you three hours of free parking. The Beverly Center at La Cienega Boulevard and Third Street has neon escalators that ascend five floors of stores and theaters. The highly attractive Santa Monica Mall has a pedestrian-only street lined with stores and sidewalk cafés. The enclosed area features a score of different food counters and dining at central tables.

LA's most exclusive shopping street

As with most things, **Las Vegas** is investing vast sums of money in order to become the most exciting retail experience in the world. Its enclosed malls are fabulous – resplendent with flying birds, ceilings that 'rain,' sunsets that change color, talking statues, and just about every gimmick imaginable. When it all becomes too much, you can climb aboard a gondola and be rowed from retail center to restaurant. The enormous Fashion Show Mall even has enough indoor retail space to display real automobiles.

ENTERTAINMENT

In New York, Boston, Philadelphia, Washington, Chicago, San Francisco, and Los Angeles, the **opera**, **ballet**, and **symphony concerts** are major events on the social calendar. You have to plan well ahead to get tickets for these, but it's worth the effort. Your travel agency will probably be happy to help you contact the relevant city information centers and arrange advance bookings, or you can do it yourself over the internet.

The best **theater** is still in New York, but other major cities have good repertory groups and experimental drama, particularly where there's a large university.

Nightclubs range from the spectacular extravaganzas of Las Vegas with top-flight singers and comedians, to the seedy strip joints (both male and female) of San Francisco, to quiet supper clubs with a dance band, or just a piano bar in the smarter hotels. Jazz is king in New Orleans. New comedians try out on Sunset Strip in Los Angeles or in Greenwich Village, New York. And satirical cabaret knocks everything it can lay its hands on in Chicago. In Miami's Little Havana they dance in the streets. In Texas, some of the nightclubs offer electronic bucking broncos and mud wrestling. But fashions change as fast as the light bulbs.

If you're a **movie** buff and like to be ahead of your crowd, some American movies that open in Europe in the autumn or at Christmas are released in the US during the summer.

New York Nightlife

If you could do justice to nighttime New York, you'd never have the energy to see it by day. But that's why they call it 'the city that never sleeps.' Pick up a copy of the *Village Voice*, the *New Yorker* or *Time Out New York* to find out what's happening.

Theater is still Broadway, on side streets between West 44th and 50th streets for the big shows and big ticket prices. Off-Broadway and Off-Off-Broadway shows are smaller and less expensive. Unless you need to see the season's smash hit, you can often pick up theater tickets at the box office a few days in advance (weekdays only). Head for the TKTS booth in Times Square (47th Street and Broadway) for half-price seats on the day of performance. Alternatively, buy a copy of the *New York Times* or one of the magazines mentioned above, and order tickets online or by mail.

New York is one of the world's dance capitals. As well as several excellent resident companies – the New York City Ballet, Merce Cunningham, Alvin Ailey, Paul Taylor, Dance Theater of Harlem, and the American Ballet Theater – the city also attracts some of the very best foreign companies.

Opera is almost as richly endowed, with the huge classical resources of the Met and the more modern repertoire of the New

Blues legend Buddy Guy playing at his club in Chicago

York City Opera, both at Lincoln Center. The New York Philharmonic is the flagship for the 30 or so classical music concerts held on any one evening – with the added summer delight of free Philharmonic and Metropolitan Opera performances in the city's parks. Cinema is also well provided for in Manhattan.

The Film Society of Lincoln Center features programs of film retrospectives and hosts the autumn New York Film Festival.

On the nightclub scene, which only really livens up after midnight, there is a wealth of music, especially in the clubs in Greenwich Village, the Meatpacking District, and on the Lower East Side. For a quieter night, go dancing under the stars at a supper club in one of the hotels around Rockefeller Center.

Washington Nightlife

The Kennedy Center for the Performing Arts is Washington's cultural star. In a beautiful location on the banks of the Potomac River, it is also the country's most prolific entertainment venue, with more than 3,000 performances held in its five theaters.

The National Symphony is a first-class orchestra. The National Theatre, which opened in 1835, stages Broadway hits and one-man performances by the famous.

For tickets, pick up an out-of-town copy of the *Washington Post* before you arrive – ideally the Friday edition with the 'Weekend' section – to plan and book ahead. Otherwise you can try for returned tickets at the box office an hour before curtain time.

San Francisco Nightlife

For nightlife, San Francisco is much more fun than Los Angeles. Los Angelenos tend to entertain at home in private, but San Franciscans go out a lot, and the coffeehouses and streets are bouncing with vitality most nights.

Bars in San Francisco are a whole way of life – Downtown Irish bars on Geary, Italian coffeehouses in North Beach, and a host of late-night waterfront 'joints' along Embarcadero to Fisherman's Wharf. There is no obvious distinction to be made between 'tourist traps' and local hangouts, perhaps because San Franciscans are enthusiastic tourists in their own town, so you'll be mixing with the locals wherever you go. Some bar-cafés around North Beach specialize in good amateur opera singing – you'll hear it as you walk by. If it sounds like Pavarotti or Callas, it probably is – played on the jukebox between 'sets.' The San Francisco Opera is very good, but you'll need to book ahead for a seat.

A friendly face behind the bar

Broadway is also the main thoroughfare for jazz clubs and various strip joints. The South of Market District, or SoMa, is home to a dynamic club scene; you'll be able to dance the night away in places that stay open until the sun comes up.

Calendar of Events

Third Monday in January Martin Luther King Day (celebrated on January 15 in some states).

Last Sunday in January Super Bowl Sunday. The climax fo the American football season is one of the biggest sporting events in the US.

February Chinese New Year (the starting date varies). Celebrations go on for a week. The largest parades are in San Francisco.

February 2 Groundhog Day. The groundhog wakes up from the winter, and goes outside to see if his shadow is visible. If it is, there will be six more weeks of winter and he goes back to sleep. Otherwise, spring is just around the corner.

Third Monday in February Presidents' Day (celebrated on February 22 in some states).

March Mardi Gras, also known as Shrove Tuesday, is 46 days before Easter, so usually falls in February or March. The celebrations in New Orleans are legendary, but the festival is celebrated with much enthusiasm and revelry all along the southern Gulf Coast.

March Spring break. Students descend on Florida for beach-based partying.

March 17 St Patrick's Day. Celebrated all over America, the largest events are in New York and Savannah.

Last Monday in May Memorial Day, to commemorate fallen servicemen and women.

June 14 Flag Day.

July 4 Independence Day. Celebrated with barbecues, picnics, family gatherings, and spectacular fireworks displays in cities across the US.

First Monday in September Labor Day.

September 17 Constitution Day.

Second Monday in October Columbus Day, also called Discoverer's Day.

October 24 United Nations Day.

October 31 Halloween. The biggest celebrations with the gaudiest costumes are in New York and San Francisco.

November 11 Veterans' Day.

Fourth Thursday in November Thanksgiving Day, to commemorate the Pilgrims' survival of their first hard year in the New World.

EATING OUT

America is a country of cuisines as diverse as its ethnic groups. Texas draws on its Mexican beginnings for spicy chili and bar-becued dishes, whilst Florida takes inspiration from Cuban rice dishes and Jewish delicatessens. Still, from Maine in the Northeast to the state of Washington in the Northwest, you'll often find simi-lar vegetable soups, plain green salads, steak and potatoes, fruit pies, and ice cream – a unity of taste that guarantees the success of fast-food franchises. Some areas do have distinctive cuisines, however, notably New York, New England, Miami, New Orleans, California, and the Pacific Northwest.

A note for Europeans – genetically modified food is very com-mon in the US and is not labeled. Foods that are not labeled as 'organic,' especially fast foods, are often GM.

What to Eat

Sandwiches. Usually served on white, rye, pumpernickel, or wholewheat bread, a roll or a bagel, or perhaps a *pita*. Classic fillings include chicken, tuna, and egg salads; lox (smoked salmon) and cream cheese served on a bagel; corned beef or pastrami (a kind of cured beef). Club sandwiches consist of three slices of toast in layers filled with turkey, lettuce, tomato, bacon, and sometimes cheese. Hoagies, heroes, submarines, po-boys, and grinders all refer to the same thing: a fat, mouth-stretching sand-wich of French bread, stuffed with meatballs, sausages, or ham-cheese-salami-onions-lettuce-peppers-tomatoes, and olive oil.

Soups. Vichyssoise is a chilled soup of leeks, potatoes, onions and cream that originated in New York; another classic Ameri-can soup is clam chowder, a New England favorite.

Salads. Many American-style restaurants feature a self-service salad bar with an attractive assortment of greens, garnishes, and

A cheerful facade in San Francisco's Haight-Ashbury district

Steak is always a winner

breads. Your choice of dressings may include 'tomatoey' French, Thousand Islands (mayonnaise, ketchup, hard-boiled egg), Russian (mayonnaise and chili sauce), Italian (oil, vinegar, garlic, and herbs), or Roquefort.

The 'chef's salad,' which may contain ham, cheese, and chicken, is a meal in itself; raw spinach salad with mushrooms ranks as a great American classic; Caesar salad has romaine lettuce, Roquefort cheese, and a raw egg in the dressing; coleslaw often appears with sandwiches. Cold pasta salads served with crisp raw vegetables or seafood are also very popular.

Meat. Beef still takes first place – it comes in enormous portions and is almost invariably tender. In steakhouses, you often pay a flat rate for a steak, a baked potato with sour cream or French fries, a self-service salad bar, and in some cases a glass or two of wine or beer.

Fish and seafood. Fish and shellfish are often of excellent quality, both the ocean fish of the East and West coasts and the Gulf of Mexico and the freshwater fish of the mountain rivers and lakes. Look out especially for red snapper, bluefish, marlin, and swordfish. Great seafoods include soft-shell and steamer crabs (especially from Maryland), Dungeness crab and Maine lobster.

Vegetables. In these health-conscious days, organic vegetables are plentiful, and excellent farmed produce is widely available. Specialty stores and restaurants open almost every week, offering vegetarian, vegan, and gluten- or dairy-free options catering to most budgets.

Cheese. Swiss-, Dutch-, and British-style cheeses are manufactured in Wisconsin, New York, and Vermont; the sharper ones approach their European equivalents. The French cheeses, imported or locally imitated, tend to be too pasteurized to approximate their taste on the other side of the Atlantic, but the creamier versions are spiced with herbs and garlic. Cheese boards are often served in French restaurants, and cheese-and-wine bars are spreading.

Desserts. Ice cream is where America excels. Amazing flavors are constantly being invented, and the range tickles any sweet tooth – spearmint, peanut butter, apple pie, cinnamon – and the vanilla is often terrific too. Put it on fruit pies, *à la mode*, and you're heading for a blissful calorific catastrophe.

Other popular American desserts include Apple Brown Betty, a kind of crumble, chocolate brownies, and various pies, including apple pie, cherry pie, pecan pie, and rich chocolate Mississippi mud pie. In early summer when the strawberries are at their peak, strawberry shortcake – scone-like biscuit on the bottom with dollops of whipped cream on top – can be sublime.

Casual dining in Seattle's Pike Place Market

Regional Cuisine

Some of the best **New York** restaurants are in the theater district, the East Side, Upper West Side, or in trendy SoHo and TriBeCa. But rather than be told where to go *this* year, just consider the variety.

A friendly restaurateur

The city benefits enormously from its cosmopolitan tradition. Italian restaurants are legion. With French eateries, you have to choose carefully between the few authentic – and very expensive – establishments and run-of-the-mill operations. Chinese places are much more reliably competent, especially in Chinatown itself. There are Greek, Spanish, Japanese, Jewish, Mexican, Brazilian, and Indian restaurants, too. Increasingly, ethnic food is being taken out on to the streets, where you'll find Arab *falafel* sandwiches, spicy Indian *samosas,* or Turkish *shish-kebab* in hot competition with the local pretzels and hot dogs.

New York's own contribution to the world of gastronomy begins with the hot dog, which you can have either with sauerkraut or fried onions but not, authentically, without mustard. The deli sandwich is a special Broadway institution, with various permutations involving turkey, corned beef, pastrami, bacon, lettuce, and tomato. New York strip steak is a good, thick cut of tenderloin, best eaten rare. Long Island Blue Point oysters are too good to spoil with the cocktail sauce that inevitably accompanies them. Manhattan clam chowder has tomato in it (as opposed to the creamy New England type). Although cheesecake may have come from Central Europe, it never tasted better than it does in Brooklyn and the delis on Broadway.

New Englanders are proud of their culinary specialties. In **Boston**, start your day with some of the 'home-baked' muffins offered at breakfast time. Blueberry, cranberry, apple, and date nut are among the more interesting varieties. Or breakfast on pancakes swimming in maple syrup. By all means be sure to try Boston baked beans. Simmered in molasses with a chunk of salt pork, the best versions of this hearty favorite have been cooked for an entire day, preferably in a brick oven.

Lovers of seafood should be sure to sample the lobster freshly caught off the coasts of Maine and Massachusetts. They are delicious boiled or steamed with melted butter, or grilled on a barbecue. Local oysters, too, are excellent, as are the haddock, sea bass, flounder, and scrod (a type of white fish, usually young cod).

For dessert, as in the rest of America, fruit pies are legion, but cranberry pie is a New England innovation. Boston cream pie is actually a sponge cake filled with custard and glazed with chocolate icing. For real local authenticity, try Indian pudding, made from cornmeal, molasses, and milk.

Thanksgiving

The fourth Thursday in November is one of the most significant holidays on the US calendar. It commemorates the the Pilgrim Fathers' successful harvest after the first hard winter. Although there is some doubt as to the historical accuracy, Thanksgiving has an affirming resonance of the original pioneering spirit. As a time for families to gather from all over the country or the globe, Thanksgiving is more important than Christmas for many Americans.

Festive food traditionally centers around roast turkey with chestnut stuffing, gravy, and cranberry sauce. Winter vegetables – sprouts, parsnips, and potatoes – are usually served as an accompaniment. There is no traditional drink, but dessert is almost always pumpkin pie.

'Floribbean' is a blend of Florida, Caribbean, and Latin flavors popular in **Miami**. When not dabbling in Floribbean, everyone eats Cuban, either *carne asada* (roasted pork) or *piccadillo* (minced beef with peppers and olives), served with earthy Cuban black beans and *yuca*, a starchy root vegetable.

New Orleans prides itself on some of the most distinctive cooking traditions in America. They certainly are evocative of the city's own personality – or could it be that the city derives its personality from the cuisine: rich, Latin, and spicy?

There are two culinary styles particular to New Orleans and Louisiana: Creole and Cajun. The Creole tradition combines a French love of intricate sauces, the Spanish penchant for mixing fish, meat, and vegetables with rice, and a taste for liberal seasoning with hot peppers developed in the West Indies and Africa.

Gumbo, a West African word for okra (known elsewhere as 'lady's fingers'), is the basic ingredient in and the generic name for thick soups of chicken or seafood. Crayfish, pronounced and often spelled in Louisiana 'crawfish,' best served straight boiled, is a favorite springtime shellfish to which whole festivals are devoted in April or May. Oysters here are plentiful and relatively inexpensive, encouraging New Orleans chefs to prepare them in numerous and marvelous ways: fried or in gumbo; as oysters Rockefeller – rich as its name implies, baked with spinach and breadcrumbs; oysters Bienville, cooked in white wine with shrimp, mushrooms, and shallots; or oysters *en brochette*, oysters skewered and wrapped in bacon. They're equally tasty eaten raw.

Cajun cooking is country-style cuisine, traditionally favored among the fishermen and farmers of the bayou. Fish soups like the spicy *courtbouillon*, spicy sausages like *boudin* and *andouille*, and world-famous *jambalaya* are classic Cajun dishes. Jambalaya is a *paella*-like dish of rice and chicken, crab, or shrimp with bits of

Acadian connection

The name 'Cajun' refers to descendants of French-Canadians, and is a contraction of 'Acadian.'

Crab claws have a devoted following in Florida

sausage or ham, pepper, and tomato. The poor man's version is the deliciously filling red beans 'n' rice, which is red kidney beans and rice flavored with pork.

The local variation on the all-American submarine sandwich is the 'po-boy' (long) or muffuletta (round) – French bread stuffed with cold meats, oysters, or other seafood, cheese, and salad, often pepped up with spice and too big for one person to finish.

Figure-conscious **California** is where healthy eating first became popular. Using the huge variety of locally produced ingredients, the state came up with 'California cuisine,' which emphasizes both freshness and simplicity and at the same time represents California's melting-pot culture.

The **Pacific Northwest** has an abundance of superb fresh ingredients, from vegetables and fruits to meat, fish, and seafood, and, in the big cities of Seattle and Portland, enough varieties of cuisines to serve them all at their best advantage. There are also wonderful ethnic influences to draw culinary inspiration from, including Europe, Canada, and the whole of the Pacific Rim.

Don't leave San Francisco without trying sourdough bread

The result is fusion – a mouthwatering menu of culinary melodies with themes from Japan and Southeast Asia as well as from French Canada and the United States. What they all have in common is the light touch that allows the excellent ingredients to shine through. That and the salmon. Copper River, wood-smoked – there are more kinds of salmon here than you can shake a rod at. Be aware, though, that two varieties of the popular sockeye salmon are listed as endangered or threatened.

Ethnic Food

Nearly every large city has its Little Italy, Chinatown, neighborhood Jewish-style delicatessen, or Mexican restaurants.

On the West Coast, particularly in San Francisco, you'll find a wonderful **Italian** version of bouillabaisse, a thick fish soup known as *cioppino*, more fish than soup, with every available shellfish spiced up or down, according to taste. Pizza is ubiquitous throughout the United States, but – thick crust or thin – its style changes from region to region.

Chinese restaurants offer many variations of Chinese regional cooking – Peking, Szechwan, Shanghai, Hunan, as well as the familiar Cantonese. It's worth calling up a day in advance to order a whole Peking duck, glazed with honey and roasted slowly with spring onions. This gentle delicacy finds a sharp contrast in the spicy smoked duck you might try in a Szechwan or Hunan restaurant.

Don't overlook seafood, such as steamed sea bass, prepared with green onions, black beans, garlic, ginger, and sesame oil, or Szechwan shrimp, served hot in both senses of the word.

Thai and **Vietnamese** restaurants have sprung up from coast to coast, offering subtler, spicier variations on the well-known Asian staples of rice and noodles. In Thai houses look out for the spicy fish dishes, delicious green curries, and soups ranging from delicately aromatic to devastatingly hot.

Japanese cuisine, particularly sushi, has made its mark all over the US. Perfectly cut yellowfin, salmon, smoked eel, and tuna, accompanied with *sake* (Japanese rice wine) is winning friends all over the States. Also look out for Japanese noodle bars and *teriaki* (a marinade used for fish, seafood, meat, or poultry).

Mexican cantinas offer an array of crispy *tacos* and *tostadas* and moist *tortillas* stuffed with shredded beef or chicken, grated cheese, avocado, and lettuce. These casual dishes tend to be 'Tex-Mex' rather than authentic Mexican, but are nevertheless very tasty. Genuine south-of-the-border dishes served in most US restaurants are more sophisticated and substantial, such as *mole poblano* (chicken with almonds, sesame seeds, peanuts, chilis, raisins, and savory chocolate sauce).

Jewish food features Eastern European borscht, cabbage soups (red or green) with sour cream, gefilte fish, and minced fish balls. Blintzes, a crisper version of the Russian blini, are folded over minced meat as an appetizer or sweet cream cheese as a dessert. Corned beef and spicy, smoked, Romanian-style pastrami are delicious in sandwiches; they are served on rye bread with potato salad and pickled cucumbers.

What to Drink

Seattle – the birthplace of Starbucks – was the town that re-defined the coffee ritual the world over. Typically, Portland claims to have pioneered the path in the gourmet coffee business, but that could just be an example of an old Portland-Seattle rivalry. Either way, both towns have innumerable small independent 'boutique' coffee shops, where you can try dozens of varieties of beans, blends, and roasts, espressos, mochas, and lattes without ever having to step into a chain outlet.

Cold drinks are invariably served iced. If you want a good serving of cola or lemonade in the coffee shops and fast-food places, specify 'little ice.' Beer is, of course, also served ice cold, (but without the ice).

Wines from California have gained acceptance worldwide. The days are long past when a Napa, Sonoma, or Anderson Valley winery was considered an upstart by French sommeliers. Fine wines from Northern California are now well established on wine lists and menus. Oregon is also making news in the wine business, particularly with some high-end reds. Be prepared for some surprisingly high prices in restaurants, though. Sometimes a good French, Italian, or Spanish wine can be less expensive on the wine list than a comparable or indifferent American offering. You can order domestic wines by the bottle or, in many places, by carafes or single glasses as the 'house wine.'

Since Americans have discovered wine, hard liquor has diminished in fashion – but not the cocktail hour. Every city has a huge number of cocktail bars, and now many established bars have cocktail menus. Dry Martinis (gin or vodka and a few drops of dry vermouth) can be potent. Bourbon, a mellow whiskey from Kentucky or Tennessee, is made of corn, malt, and rye; drink it straight, on the rocks, or with soda. Many bars promote late-afternoon 'happy hours' when two drinks are served for the price of one. Another attraction for spirit-drinkers is that American bartenders often serve very friendly measures.

New Orleans claims to have invented the cocktail, or at least the word. It is, they say, a distortion of the French for eggcup, *coquetier*, in which a Creole bartender by the name of Antoine Peychaud served his brandy and bitters in the 19th century. The dictionary, a little more soberly, suggests that cocktail was originally 'a horse of racing qualities, but not a thoroughbred.' That could also serve as a fair description of two local specialties: the Sazarac is rye whiskey or bourbon and bitters served in a glass coated with anisette; the Ramos Gin Fizz adds sugar, lemon, lime, orange-flower water, egg white, crushed ice, and soda water to the gin. If you're still conscious, try a *café brûlot*, coffee flavored with cinnamon, cloves, orange peel, and *flambé*.

American beers have also risen above the gassy, industrial, canned brews of old. Brewpubs and microbreweries have sprung up all over the country. Treats are in store for fans of the fermented hop from Washington state to California, and all the way across America to New York state.

Beer fans will find much to enjoy stateside

HANDY TRAVEL TIPS

An A–Z Summary of Practical Information

A

ACCOMMODATIONS

Hotels and motels. It's always wise to make reservations in advance, and you can do this directly through the nationwide toll-free reservation services operated by the large hotel and motel chains (listed in the telephone directory or on www.yellowbook.com).

American hotels and motels usually charge by the room, not by the number of occupants. Rates indicated normally do not include the state and city sales taxes or daily occupancy tax. Most rooms have air-conditioning, a private bathroom, and a television.

You normally have the choice of twin or double beds, and motel rooms often have two double beds – convenient for family travel. Many resort hotels offer special rates to guests who take their meals on the premises.

Motels are one of America's bargains. Many belong to national chains, so you can book an entire cross-country trip in one go.

Country inns. These are often large, luxurious, older, but beautifully restored properties. Guests tend to stay for more than just one night and dinner is a fairly formal affair, usually eaten with the other residents in the dining room. Country inns can be expensive.

Guest houses and bed-and-breakfast inns. These tend to be fancier and pricier than their European counterparts and are found in smaller towns and holiday centers. Local tourist authorities have extensive lists.

Ranches. Ranches in America can mean far more than just cowboys, campfires, and horses. There are luxury ranches, enormous complexes with all facilities including swimming pools and tennis courts, and the simpler – but nevertheless comfortable – dude ranches, where guests take part in everyday life. For further information, contact a travel agency, or try www.duderanch.org. Budget accommodations can be found on farms and family ranches; local tourist authorities have lists.

AIRPORTS (See also GETTING TO THE USA)

Boston: Logan International (BOS) is 3 miles (5km) east of the business district. An airport bus service to major hotels runs every 30 minutes during the day; travel time 20–30 minutes. A shuttle-bus service (Massport) runs to the subway (Blue Line) every 15 minutes during the day; travel time 15 minutes. There are also shared-ride van services to Boston and surrounding towns. A free airport bus to the Water Shuttle runs every 15 minutes during daylight across Inner Harbor to Downtown Boston. The subway and Water Shuttle are recommended over car or bus due to frequent traffic jams at Sumner Tunnel.

Chicago: O'Hare International (ORD) is 18 miles (29km) northwest of the Loop. A bus service to Downtown hotels runs every 10 minutes during the day. The CTA Blue Line subway runs every 15–30 minutes during the day, every 60 minutes at night. You can transfer to Midway Airport (MDW) using Omega Airport Shuttle.

Los Angeles: Los Angeles International (LAX) is 16 miles (26km) south of the central business district. The FlyAway airport bus service runs to Union Station in Downtown Los Angeles, where connections can be made to surrounding areas. Private door-to-door shuttles are also available, tel: 1-800-650-8441 or 1-800-400-8060. You can also transfer to Van Nuys Airport (VNY) via FlyAway.

Miami: Miami International (MIA) is 7 miles (11.5km) west of Downtown Miami. The Super Shuttle minibus service is available from arrivals, tel: 305-871-2000. Municipal buses run from the airport bus station (on the first level of concourse E, opposite US Customs) to Miami and Miami Beach; however, there is no luggage space provided. Transfer by coach to Fort Lauderdale Airport (FLL) takes around 60 minutes, depending on traffic.

New York area: John F. Kennedy International (JFK) is 15 miles (24km) southeast of Midtown Manhattan. The AirTrain (www.jfk airtrain.com) runs 24 hours to Howard Beach and Jamaica stations where you can connect with the subway to Manhattan (60 mins) or Long Island Rail Road (LIRR) to Penn Station (35 mins). Super

Shuttle runs 24 hours to any Manhattan destination, and the New York Airport Service runs to Midtown hotels between 31st and 60th. Taxis cost a $45 flat rate, not including tolls or tip, to or from any destination below 96th Street in Manhattan.

Newark Airport (NWR) is located in New Jersey, 16 miles (26km) from Midtown Manhattan. The AirTrain takes you to Newark Liberty AirTrain station, where you can take a NJ Transit commuter train to New York's Penn Station (30 mins). Taxis to Manhattan take 30–45 minutes; the metered fare usually runs at around $55, not including tolls and tip. The Newark Liberty Airport Express shuttle runs to 34th Street/Eighth Avenue, the Port Authority Bus Terminal on 42nd Street, or an east-side terminal on 41st Street (between Third and Lexington).

LaGuardia Airport (LGA) is located in Queens, 8 miles (13km) from Midtown Manhattan. Taxis cost about $25, not including tolls or tip; the ride in takes about 30–40 minutes. Shuttles include SuperShuttle and New York Airport Service. The M60 bus connects LaGuardia with the subways in Manhattan; Q33 and Q48 buses connect with the subway in Queens; the trip takes longer than a taxi but is much cheaper.

San Francisco: San Francisco International (SFO) is 14 miles (22km) south of Downtown near the town of San Mateo. The Bay Area Rapid Transit system (BART) has a metro rail stop at the airport, with some trains going all the way into the center of the city. Other services connect to this line, providing access to the Bay Area. BART also connects with CalTrain, which serves Silicon Valley towns like San Jose.

BUDGETING FOR YOUR TRIP

On the whole, the US is an inexpensive place to visit. With a huge choice of accommodations, nightlife, and places to eat, it's easy to satisfy most budgets. Las Vegas is a real bargain, as the casinos use cheap hotel deals, drinks, and all-you-can-eat buffets as a lure to get people to their gaming tables. Hotels in New York, Washington, Los Angeles, and San Francisco are not bargains, however, so you'll need to shop around and book in advance.

Flights from the UK to the US are most expensive in July and August, when a round-trip ticket to LA can easily cost £800. Savvy savers visit New York in November and early December (avoid Thanksgiving – the fourth Thursday in November), when the city is blazing with Christmas lights and the shopping is excellent, or Florida in February, for winter sunshine. Discounted fares are available online from £250–350.

Car hire is inexpensive, and fly-drive packages, especially attractive if visiting Florida, bring the price down even more. US gasoline is cheap by European standards.

Entrance to all 19 museums which make up the Smithsonian Institute (most in Washington, DC) are free, but most major museums and attractions charge admission of around $12–$20.

Orlando's theme parks can be expensive, especially if you don't plan ahead. Prices at Walt Disney World Resort are from $30 a day for anyone aged 10 and above, or from $24 aged three to nine. The longer you stay, the less you pay, however, so a seven-day ticket is a better deal.

America's glorious national parks and monuments are the country's best bargains. Historic attractions like the Alamo in Texas and Philadelphia's Liberty Bell are free, while entry to the parks themselves is minimal: California's Yosemite charges $20 per family car, with unlimited access for seven days; Arizona's Grand Canyon is $25 per car. If you plan to visit several parks, invest in an America the Beautiful – National Parks and Federal Lands Annual Pass, for only $80.

C

CAMPING

Camping in America generally involves some kind of recreational vehicle – campers, motorhomes, or trailers (caravans), although in some areas you are allowed just to arrive and pitch a tent. Campgrounds are divided into two categories: public (found in the national parks, state parks, and state forests) and private. Almost all facilities have running water; some even have restaurants. Sites in the most popular parks must be booked directly with the individual lodge, anywhere from eight weeks to a year in advance, depending on the season. If you are sleeping in a tent, you must obtain a permit from the park.

CAR RENTAL

Most car-rental companies offer a flat rate with unlimited mileage. If you are planning to drive more than 70 miles (112km) a day, this is probably the solution for you. Charges vary, so shop around for the best deal. There are also companies specializing in older, worn, but mechanically sound cars. They can be less expensive and good for local touring. If you're traveling during the summer months, be sure your car has air-conditioning. You may also want to look into rent-here, leave-there deals.

Car-rental companies include: Alamo (www.goalamo.com), Avis (www.avis.com), Budget (www.budget.com), Dollar (www.dollar. com), Enterprise (www.enterprise.com), Hertz (www.hertz.com), National (www.nationalcar.com), and Thrifty (www.thrifty.com).

A major credit card is essential to avoid paying an enormous deposit; some companies even refuse to accept cash as a deposit. For tourists from non-English-speaking countries, a translation of your driver's license is highly recommended, together with the national license itself, or an International Driving Permit.

Auto driveaway. If you'd like a budget way to cross the country, look into an auto-driveaway deal. Several companies engage people to drive cars from one part of the country to a specified destination. A refundable security deposit and an International Driving Permit are required, and the driver must be at least 21 years old. You pay gasoline (petrol) expenses yourself, and you have to take a reasonably direct route established in advance. Consult the telephone directory (www.yellowbook.com) or visit www.autodriveaway.com.

CLIMATE AND CLOTHING

In summer, it's warm everywhere except northern New England, Oregon, and Washington. One city anomaly is San Francisco, where spring and summer can be surprisingly chilly. In winter, heavy outer wear is essential, except in the southernmost states. For New York and Chicago, rubber overshoes are a good idea. Even in Florida and California, temperatures can be freezing in winter, but cold spells never last long. Have a sweater handy for chilly air-conditioned temperatures indoors.

Monthly daytime temperatures in degrees Fahrenheit:

		J	F	M	A	M	J	J	A	S	O	N	D
Chicago	max	32	35	45	59	70	81	84	83	76	65	48	35
	min	17	20	29	40	50	60	65	64	56	46	33	22
LA	max	67	68	69	71	73	77	83	84	83	78	73	68
	min	47	49	50	53	56	60	64	64	63	59	52	48
Miami	max	76	77	80	83	85	88	89	90	88	85	80	77
	min	59	59	63	67	71	74	76	76	75	71	65	60
NY	max	39	40	48	61	71	81	85	83	77	67	54	41
	min	26	27	34	44	53	63	68	66	60	51	41	30

And in degrees Celsius:

		J	F	M	A	M	J	J	A	S	O	N	D
Chicago	max	0	2	7	15	21	27	29	28	24	18	9	2
	min	-8	-7	-2	5	10	16	18	18	13	8	1	-6
LA	max	19	20	21	22	23	25	28	29	28	26	23	20
	min	8	10	10	12	13	16	18	18	17	15	11	9
Miami	max	24	25	27	28	29	31	32	32	31	29	27	25
	min	15	15	17	19	22	23	24	24	23	22	18	16
NY	max	4	5	9	16	22	27	29	28	25	19	12	5
	min	-3	-3	1	7	12	17	20	19	16	11	5	-1

CONSULATES

Every major US city has consulates to serve foreign nationals. The following are in New York. Consult the phone book for those in other cities.

Australia: 150 East 42nd Street, Floor 34, New York 10017, tel: 212-351-6500, www.australianyc.org.

Canada: 1251 Avenue of the Americas (at 50th Street) New York, NY 10019, tel: 212-596-1628.

Ireland: 345 Park Avenue (at 51st Street), New York, NY 10022, tel: 212-319-2555, www.consulateofirelandnewyork.org.

New Zealand: 780 Third Avenue, New York, NY 10017, tel: 212-832-4038.

South Africa: 333 East 38th Street, New York 10016, tel: 212-213-4880, www.southafrica-newyork.net.

UK: 845 Third Avenue, New York, NY 10022, tel: 212-986-2200, http://ukinusa.fco.gov.uk.

CRIME AND SAFETY

Crime rates are falling in many major American cities. Petty theft and non-violent crime are still commonplace though, and violent crimes still occur. Follow a few common-sense rules, relax and enjoy yourself. Keep valuables, cash, and travelers' checks in a hotel safe. Carry only what you need from day to day. Be sure your bag is securely fastened, and keep your wallet in an inside rather than hip pocket. Never leave belongings unattended – at an airport, in a store, on the beach, or on view in a car. As in most countries, be on the alert for pickpockets and bag-snatchers in any crowded area.

If you are in unfamiliar territory, inquire if any neighborhoods are unsafe. After dark, stay where the crowds are. If you are driving, keep car doors locked and windows up to prevent someone entering when you're stopped at a traffic light. By the same token, never drive around with the windows wide open and your purse or valuables on the passenger seat.

CUSTOMS AND ENTRY REQUIREMENTS

Many foreign visitors need a visitor's visa, which can be obtained at any US embassy or consulate. Visitors from the UK, Australia, New Zealand, Singapore, and some European countries qualify for the visa-waiver program, and therefore do not need a visa for stays of less than 90 days, as long as they have a valid 10-year machine-readable passport and a return ticket. Visitors who qualify for the visa-waiver program must apply online for authorization at least 72 hours before traveling at https://esta.cbp.dhs.gov.

As security measures become stricter, be prepared to be finger-printed and photographed on arrival. Everyone must fill out customs declaration forms (usually distributed by your airline near the end of the flight). For a breakdown of up-to-date US Customs and Border Protection regulations, go to www.cbp.gov.

A non-resident may bring, free of duty and taxes, articles up to $100 in value for use as gifts for other people. This exemption is valid only if the gifts accompany you in your luggage, if you stay 72 hours or more, and have not claimed this exemption within the preceding six months. Up to 100 cigars may be included within this gift exemption, but Cuban cigars are illegal.

Plants and foodstuffs also are subject to strict control; visitors from abroad may not import fruits, vegetables, or meat.

Arriving and departing passengers are required to report any money or checks, etc., exceeding a total of $10,000.

D

DRIVING

Drive on the right. Intersections are generally marked with stop or yield signs to indicate who has priority. Speed limits vary from state to state, and depend on the type of road on which you are traveling. The speed limits range between 75mph (120km/h) on some states' freeways and 15mph (24km/h) in some school zones. These limits are almost always clearly posted, and are strictly enforced, as are stop signs.

An excellent interstate highway system crosses the US. Odd numbers designate highways running north–south, while even-numbered interstates run east–west.

If you have a breakdown on a freeway, pull over onto the right-hand shoulder, turn on your hazard lights, tie a white cloth to the door handle or radio aerial, raise the hood (bonnet), and either use your cellphone to call for help or wait in the car for assistance.

American Automobile Association. The AAA (1000 AAA Drive, Heathrow, Florida 32746-5603, tel: 1-800-AAA-HELP (222-4357); www.aaa.com) offers lots of information on traveling in the US, as well as short-term insurance for visitors. The AAA also helps members, as well as foreign visitors affiliated with recognized automobile associations, in case of breakdown or other problems.

Gasoline (petrol) and services. Stations are numerous and easy to locate. Many stations might be closed in the evenings and on weekends. At night, some gas stations require exact change or a credit card. No tipping is required for 'full-service,' though the per gallon price is often higher.

E

ELECTRICITY

110-volt 60-cycle AC is standard throughout the US. Plugs are the flat, two- and three-pronged variety. Visitors from abroad will need a transformer (240–110V) and an adapter plug for their electric razors, etc, unless they are the dual-voltage type.

EMERGENCIES

In the States, you should call **911** for all emergencies – fire, police, ambulance, and paramedics.

G

GAY AND LESBIAN TRAVELERS

The unofficial gay capital of America (some say the world) is San Francisco, and specifically the area called The Castro. The gay and lesbian community has made significant inroads into local politics, and unlike in most of the US, same-sex marriage (currently legal only in Massachusetts and Connecticut) is a live issue.

Most cities have a gay quarter, but New York, Miami, New Orleans, and the West Hollywood area of Los Angeles are particularly receptive. Halloween in New York and San Francisco, and Mardi Gras in New Orleans, are always riotous events. Los Angeles is the home of the ONE National Gay and Lesbian Archives (www.one archives.org), the world's largest research library.

GETTING TO THE USA

Scheduled flights. New York is the principal gateway to the US from the UK, but major transatlantic carriers offer direct flights from Heathrow and Gatwick to many other US destinations, including Boston, Miami, Chicago, Dallas/Fort Worth, Los Angeles, and San Francisco. Direct flights are also available from Ireland. Flying time from London to New York is 7 hours, to Los Angeles, 11 hours.

From Sydney and Auckland, scheduled flights leave daily for Los Angeles, with connections to other US cities. Direct flights are also available from most other countries; some Europeans find it less expensive to fly from their country to Britain to take advantage of the cheaper US flights that depart from the UK.

Aside from the standard fares, many other types are available. Consult an airline, the internet, or a travel agency for the latest information about discounts and special fares.

Package holidays. A wide variety are available, ranging from fully organized to flexible. Some packages include the rental cost of a car, a RV (motorhome), or camping equipment.

Baggage. You are allowed to check in, free of charge, two suitcases of normal size on scheduled transatlantic flights. In addition, one piece of hand baggage of a size that fits easily under the aircraft seat may be carried on board. If in doubt, check size and weight restrictions with your travel agent or air carrier when booking your ticket. Many American carriers now make a charge per suitcase on internal flights not related to your transatlantic flight. It is advisable to insure all luggage for the duration of your trip.

GETTING AROUND THE USA

By bus. Greyhound bus lines (tel: 1-800 231-2222; www.greyhound. com) provide transportation to and from cities all over the United States. Passengers can make as many stopovers en route as they wish, provided the destination is reached before the ticket expires.

Sometimes travel by bus costs about the same – or even more – than flying; don't automatically assume the bus is less expensive. Flat-rate rover passes for specified periods of unlimited travel are sometimes available, but must be purchased outside the US.

By train. Five hundred major cities and towns are linked daily by Amtrak (tel: 1-800 USA-RAIL; www.amtrak.com), America's national railroad passenger corporation. Amtrak sometimes has bargain fares, including excursion and family fares. USA Railpasses enable you to visit any destination in Amtrak's system within a 15-day, 30-day or 45-day period. Trains are a far less efficient means of transportation than in Europe – buses are usually a better option for long-distance travel, though trains are more comfortable.

By air. Air travel is by far the quickest way of getting around the US. Shuttle services operate on some heavily traveled routes, and with the emergence of 'paperless tickets,' traveling by air is as simple and straightforward as any other means of transportation. Fares change constantly, so it would be wise to consult an airline or travel agency for the latest information about discounts and special deals.

Alternatively, be on the lookout for special deals on the internet. Fares tend to be lowest midweek and during the wintertime.

Local transportation. Municipal buses operate in most cities and towns, and exact change is required. Some big cities have subway (underground rail) systems. Maps of the network are usually posted at every station and in every train, and can be obtained at the ticket booth in any station. To take the subway, you need a token or fare card (purchased at the booth), which you insert in the turnstile.

Taxis. Taxis are lined up at airports, train stations, and bus terminals, or you can hail a cab in the street or telephone for one. A tip of at least 15 percent is expected. On arrival in the US, if you take a taxi from the airport into town, make sure you have several small banknotes – 20s are best – as many cab drivers will not give change for large denominations. Always travel with branded, recognizable taxi firms – never with unlicensed cabs. Flat fares from the airport into a specific city are often posted inside the cab itself, but always get a confirmed quote before you accept a ride.

H

HEALTH AND MEDICAL CARE

Free medical service is not available in the US, and a visit to the doctor can be expensive, hospitalization an economic disaster. Payment for any medical services will be expected on the spot. Holiday medical insurance is a very wise precaution. You can arrange for coverage through one of the big international companies or your travel agent.

Pharmacies. It is generally advisable to bring with you any medicines you require regularly. Be aware that many medicines you can buy over the counter in your home country require a prescription in the US. If you need to buy prescription drugs during your stay, you will have to get a prescription from a local physician.

L

LIQUOR (ALCOHOL) REGULATIONS

Liquor laws vary from state to state and sometimes within a state. Utah is strictest, Nevada the most liberal. Some states allow alcohol to be sold in supermarkets or drugstores, in others only licensed liquor (or 'package') stores sell even beer. The sale of alcohol on Sundays and holidays (except by the glass in restaurants) is frequently restricted or prohibited.

The minimum age for purchasing alcoholic beverages is 21. You may be asked for some identification when buying alcohol or entering a nightclub that serves alcohol, whether or not you look under age, and you can be refused if you have no ID.

M

MAPS

Tourist information authorities distribute free maps and brochures. City and state maps can be purchased in bookstores and stationery stores and at many gas stations and larger supermarkets.

MEDIA

You'll almost certainly have radio and television in your hotel room, with a vast choice of programs. American commercial television aims to appeal to the largest possible number of people, while independent programmers like HBO have some of the best and most original shows. The non-commercial Public Broadcasting Service (PBS) screens music and drama programs (many of them bought from the BBC) along with its own news and information broadcasts.

There are numerous AM and FM radio stations. Most broadcast pop or country music, but each large city has at least one classical music radio station, and some have jazz stations. The highest-quality programming (including news) is generally on National Public Radio (NPR) stations.

MONEY

The dollar is divided into 100 cents. Coins: 1 (penny), 5 (nickel), 10 (dime), 25 (quarter), 50 (half-dollar), and $1. Bills: $1, $2 (rare), $5, $10, $20, $50, and $100. Larger denominations ($500 and $1,000) are not in general circulation.

All denominations are the same size and primarily green in color. The latest $5, $10, $20, and $50 bills are easier to read with some different-colored elements, but check carefully before paying.

Currency exchange. Normal banking hours are from 9am to 2pm, Monday to Friday. Only major banks in larger cities or at international airports will change foreign money or foreign-currency travelers' checks, so it's important to carry cash or travelers' checks in dollars. If you're cashing travelers' checks in a bank, be sure to take your passport. It's a good idea to have a supply of $1–$10 bills on hand for taxis, tipping, and small purchases.

Credit cards. Credit cards play an even greater role here than in Europe. In the US, they are a way of life, and most Americans have several. The major credit cards are accepted almost everywhere. When paying for goods or services, including hotel and restaurant checks, you will usually be asked: 'Cash or charge?' In some towns, like Las Vegas, you may be asked to show an ID when using your credit card.

Travelers' checks. Visitors from abroad will find travelers' checks drawn on American banks, or checks issued by American Express, far easier to deal with than those issued by local banks. Travelers' checks are widely accepted in stores, restaurants, and hotels. Only carry small amounts of cash at a time, and, if possible, keep the rest of your checks in the hotel safe.

ATMs. These are widely available; however, a withdrawal fee is usually charged, which varies from location to location. (Tip: *never* use an ATM in a casino.)

N

NATIONAL PARKS

Government-protected reserves, found all over the US, take in everything from stretches of coastland and wayside campgrounds to wildlife reserves and wilderness areas. The sites designated 'National Park' or 'National Monument' are areas of outstanding historical, geological, and scenic importance. Almost all can be reached by car, and some have direct connections to major cities by rail or air. Each state also has numerous 'State Parks,' generally of lesser consequence, although many have outstanding scenic and recreational resources.

High season is mid-July to mid-August, when the most popular parks are likely to be crowded and advance reservations for campgrounds are recommended. Entrance fees to the parks vary. The reasonably priced America the Beautiful Pass (buy it inside the parks or at http://store.usgs.gov/pass) entitles four adults in a private car to unlimited access to national parks for a year. Seniors are entitled to reduced rates.

Some of the best national parks have been dealt with in detail in this guide. Here are a few more:

Mesa Verde National Park (Colorado): Native Americans abandoned this prehistoric 'green tabletop' 800 years ago, leaving behind stone cities built into the cliffside. Over 4,000 known archeological sites are preserved here.

Petrified Forest National Park (Arizona): In the most colorful area of the Painted Desert, six forests of fallen logs, 200 million years old, have turned into jasper and agate.

Shenandoah National Park (Virginia): Nearest wilderness park to the nation's capital, this park consists of a 105-mile (170km) stretch of wooded Blue Ridge Mountains.

For further information, write to the Department of the Interior, National Park Service, 1849 C Street NW, Washington, DC 20240;

tel: 202-208-4747, or go to www.nps.gov. For state parks, write to the state tourist department or search the internet.

O

OPENING TIMES

Normal hours for offices and businesses are 9am to 5 or 6pm. Banks open Monday to Friday between 9am and 2pm, with many staying open until 4pm; some branches are open until noon on Saturdays. Major museums are generally open every day 10am to 5.30pm; smaller museums and art galleries may have varying hours and usually close one day a week, often on Mondays. Stores in city streets usually open at 9am and close at 5.30pm, but stores in shopping centers and malls stay open longer, often until about 9pm. The shopping malls inside Las Vegas's gigantic casinos are usually open until midnight.

P

POLICE (See also CRIME AND SAFETY and EMERGENCIES)

City police are concerned with local crime and traffic violations, while Highway Patrol officers (also called State Troopers) ensure road safety, and are on the lookout for people speeding or driving under the influence of alcohol or drugs.

American police officers are often fair and friendly. Do not hesitate to approach an officer to ask for assistance or information. In case of emergency, dial 911 to contact the police.

POST OFFICES

The US postal service deals only with mail; unlike in other countries, you cannot cash checks or make international telephone calls. Post office hours are from 8 or 9am to 5 or 6pm Monday to Friday, and from 8 or 9am to noon or 1pm on Saturdays. Some branches have longer hours. Smaller branches close one afternoon a week, often Wednesday; all are closed on Sunday. Stamps can also be purchased from vending machines in drugstores, and in air, rail, and bus terminals, but you will pay a surcharge.

General delivery (also known as 'poste restante'). Mail marked 'General Delivery' can be sent to you care of the main post office of any town. Letters will be held for no more than a month. American Express offices also keep mail for 30 days; envelopes should be marked 'Client's Mail.' Be sure to take a driver's license or passport for identification.

PUBLIC HOLIDAYS

The following public holidays are – with a few exceptions – celebrated nationwide.

New Year's Day	January 1
Martin Luther King Day	Third Monday in January (celebrated in most states; on January 15 in some states)
Presidents' Day or 'Washington's Birthday'	Third Monday in February (celebrated on February 22 in some states)
Memorial Day	Last Monday in May
Independence Day	July 4
Labor Day	First Monday in September
Columbus Day	Second Monday in October (celebrated in most states, on October 12 in some states)
Veterans' Day	November 11
Thanksgiving	Fourth Thursday in November
Christmas	December 25

Lincoln's Birthday (February 12) is sometimes observed in the northern states; Robert E. Lee's Birthday (January 19) and Confederate Memorial Day (late April/early May) are sometimes celebrated in southern states.

If a holiday falls on a Sunday, banks and most stores close on the following day. There are also long weekends (such as the one following Thanksgiving) when offices are closed for four days. Many restaurants never shut, however, not even at Christmas.

R

RESTROOMS

Americans use the terms 'restroom,' 'powder room,' 'bathroom' and 'ladies" or 'men's room' to indicate the toilet. If you encounter a pay-toilet, the usual charge is 25¢.

T

TELEPHONES

Many European cell (mobile) phones do not work in the States, but public telephones can be found just about everywhere. Call rates are listed and explained in the front of the general directory or White Pages. Evening (after 5pm), night (after 11pm), and weekend rates are generally lower. For Information (directory inquiries) call 411. All long-distance calls require you to punch '1' before the three-digit area code for direct service. Be aware that in some heavily populated areas, like Greater Las Vegas, it's necessary to dial the entire area code even if it's a local call with the same code. All numbers with an 800, 888, or 877 prefix are toll-free. Always dial 1 before the 800.

Long-distance and many international calls may be dialed direct, but are very expensive at pay phones. You can save money with a phone card bought from a drugstore.

TIME ZONES

The 48 contiguous states of the US are – from east to west – divided into four time zones: Eastern (GMT -5 hours), Central (-6), Mountain (-7), and Pacific (-8). The major part of Alaska is on GMT -9 hours, and Hawaii is on GMT -10. Under Daylight Saving Time, observed in all states except Hawaii and parts of Arizona, clocks move ahead one hour on the second Sunday in March and turn back again the first Sunday in November.

TIPPING

In general, a service charge is not included in the bill; you are expected to tip the waiter, waitress, or bartender about 15 percent (more in New York City or luxury establishments). Movie house or theater ushers are not tipped, but doormen, cloakroom attendants, etc., should be remunerated – never less than a quarter.

Here are some more tipping suggestions:

Bell hop (porter)	$1–$2 per bag
Hotel maid (not for single night)	$1–$2 per day
Restroom attendant	50¢ minimum
Taxi driver	15 percent
Bus tour guide	10–15 percent
Hairdresser/barber	15 percent

TOURIST INFORMATION

Convention and visitors' bureaux in principal cities:

Atlanta: Convention and Visitors' Bureau, 233 Peachtree Street, NE, Suite 1400, Atlanta, GA 30303, tel: 404-521-6600; www.acvb.com

Baltimore: Convention and Visitors' Association, 100 Light Street, No. 12, Baltimore, MD 21202, tel: 410-659-7300; http://baltimore.org

Boston: Greater Boston Convention and Visitors' Bureau, Two Copley Place, Suite 105, Boston, MA 02116-6501, tel: 1-888-SEE BOSTON; www.bostonusa.com

Chicago: Office of Tourism, 2301 S. Lake Shore Drive, Chicago, IL 60616, tel: 312-567-8500; www.choosechicago.com

Dallas: Convention and Visitors' Bureau, 325 West St Paul Street, Suite 700, Dallas, TX 75201, tel: 214-571-1000; www.visitdallas.com

Denver: Metro Convention and Visitors' Bureau, 1555 California Street, Suite 300, Denver, CO 80202, tel: 1-800-338-7648; www.denver.org

Detroit: Metro Convention and Visitors' Bureau, 211 West Fort Street, Suite 1000, Detroit, MI 48226, tel: 313-202-1952; www.visitdetroit.com

Houston: Greater Houston Convention and Visitors' Bureau, 901 Bagby, Houston, TX 77002, tel: 713-227-3100; www.visithoustontexas.com

Las Vegas: Convention and Visitors' Authority, 3150 Paradise Road, Las Vegas, NV 89109, tel: 702-892-77573; www.visitlasvegas.com

Los Angeles: Hollywood Visitor Information Center, Hollywood and Highland Center, 6801 Hollywood Boulevard, Hollywood, CA, tel: 323-467-6412; www.discoverlosangeles.com

Miami/Miami Beach: Miami Convention and Visitors' Bureau, 701 Brickell Avenue, Miami, FL 33131, tel: 305-539-3000; www.miamiandbeaches.com

New Orleans: New Orleans Metropolitan Convention and Visitors' Bureau, 2020 St Charles Avenue, New Orleans, LA 70130, tel: 504-566-5011; www.neworleanscvb.com

New York: Convention and Visitors' Bureau, 810 Seventh Avenue (at 53rd Street), New York, NY 10019, tel: 212-397-8222; http://nycgo.com

Philadelphia: Convention and Visitors' Bureau, 1700 Market Street, Philadelphia, PA 19103, tel: 215-636-3300; www.philadelphiausa.travel

Phoenix: Convention and Visitors' Bureau, 400 East Van Buren Street, Suite 600, Phoenix, AZ 85004, tel: 602-254-6500; www.visitphoenix.com

Salt Lake: Convention and Visitors' Bureau, 90 South West Temple, Salt Lake City, UT 84101, tel: 801-534-4900; www.visitsaltlake.com

San Antonio: Convention and Visitors' Bureau, 203 South St Mary's Street, TX 78205, tel: 210-270-6700; www.visitsanantonio.com

San Diego: Convention and Visitors' Bureau, 2215 India Street, San Diego, CA 92101, tel: 619-232-3101; www.sandiego.org

San Francisco: Visitor Information Center, 900 Market Street, San Francisco, CA 94102-2804, tel: 415-391-2000; www.onlyinsanfrancisco.com

Santa Fe: Convention and Visitors' Bureau, 201 West Marcy Street, Santa Fe, NM 87501, tel: 505-955-6200; www.santafe.org

Seattle: Convention and Visitors' Bureau, 701 Pike Street, Suite 800, Seattle, WA 98101, tel: 206-461-5840; www.visitseattle.org

Washington, DC: Convention and Visitors' Association, 1212 New York Avenue NW, Washington, DC 20005, tel: 202-789-7000; www.washington.org

TRAVELERS WITH DISABILITIES

The American Disabilities Act requires equal access for the disabled at most places that cater to the public, including all government facilities. Amtrak, the coast-to-coast railroad, has some accessible bedrooms and occasionally offers discounted tickets.

The Society for Accessible Travel and Hospitality (SATH) has numerous resources for travelers with disabilities, including an informative website. Contact the Society for Accessible Travel and Hospitality, 347 Fifth Avenue, Suite 605, New York, New York 10016, tel: 212-447-7284, www.sath.org.

W

WEBSITES AND INTERNET CAFÉS

Internet cafés are not as common as they are in other countries, but try a document-copy store such as Kinko's, or even a public library. Wireless internet access is increasingly popular; many cafés and even entire city districts now have WiFi, if you have your own computer.

Websites for city tourist information centers can be found on *pages 247–9*. Other recommended websites include:

www.discoveramerica.com – Official travel website for the US.

www.visitusa.com – Information on beaches, hotels and attractions on a state-by-state basis.

www.discovernewengland.org – Official website for New England.

www.capitalregionusa.org – Official website for Washington, DC, Maryland and Virginia.

www.travelsouthusa.com – Representing the 12 Southern US states.

www.visitcalifornia.com – Promotes the huge variety of activities and attractions in California.

WEIGHTS AND MEASURES

The United States is one of the last countries in the world to resist the metric system. Milk and fruit juice are sold by the quart or half-gallon, but wine and spirits now come in liter bottles. Food products usually have the weight marked in kilos and grams as well as pounds and ounces.

There are some differences between British and American measures: 1 US gallon = 0.833 Imperial gallons = 3.8 liters and 1 US quart = 0.833 Imperial quarts = 0.9 liters.

YOUTH HOSTELS

These inexpensive accommodations are open to members of national youth hostel organizations. Visit the website of Hostelling International-USA at www.hiusa.org for information on membership and a list of hostels near the US town or state you want to visit.

A number of centrally located residences are run by the YMCA and the YWCA. Rates are quite reasonable. Membership is not necessary, but demand is high, so make reservations two months ahead; tel: 1-800-872-9622; or www.ymca.net.

Students and young people can find inexpensive accommodations at university campuses and through local student associations.

INDEX

Berlitz pocket guide

USA

Sixth Edition 2010

Written by Jack Altman
Updated by Martha Ellen Zenfell
Edited by Tom Stainer
Series Editor: Tony Halliday

No part of this book may be reproduced, stored in a retrieval system or transmitted in any form or means electronic, mechanical, photocopying, recording or otherwise, without prior written permission from Berlitz Publishing. Brief text quotations with use of photographs are exempted for book review purposes only.

Every effort has been made to provide accurate information in this publication, but changes are inevitable. The publisher cannot be responsible for any resulting loss, inconvenience or injury.

All Rights Reserved
© 2010 Berlitz Publishing/Apa
Publications GmbH & Co. Verlag KG,
Singapore Branch, Singapore

Printed in Singapore by Insight Print Services (Pte) Ltd, 38 Joo Koon Road, Singapore 628990. Tel: (65) 6865-1600. Fax: (65) 6861-6438

Berlitz Trademark Reg. U.S. Patent Office and other countries. Marca Registrada

Photography credits
AKG-Images London 16, 25; Pete Bennett 125; Bruce Bernstein Collection/courtesy Princeton University Library 23; Chris Coe 73, 172, 173, 175; Corbis 36; Alex Demyan 121, 122; Jerry Dennis 190; David Dunai/APA 38, 127, 131, 133, 134, 136, 206; Mary Evans 20; Jay Fechtman 43, 51, 90, 94, 213; Glyn Genin 11, 164, 165, 176, 180, 183, 188, 209, 211, 224; Tony Halliday/APA 41, 47, 56, 150, 161, 163, 186; Illustrated London News 27; iStockphoto 80, 119, 138, 141, 142, 146, 149, 181; Kerrick James 202; Britta Jaschinski/APA 52, 208; Las Vegas News Bureau 29, 194, 195; Leonardo.com 218; Eric Long/NASM 98; Anna Mockford and Nick Bonnetti/APA 10, 13, 42, 45, 49, 50, 53, 54, 57, 59, 61, 63, 64; Abe Nowitz/APA 8, 77, 196; Daniella Nowitz/APA 168, 170; Richard Nowitz/APA 6, 9, 12, 14, 15, 69, 74, 76, 79, 83, 85, 86, 89, 93, 97, 101, 105, 114, 116, 117, 144, 157, 171, 191, 204, 205, 214, 216, 220, 223; Palm Beach Tourism 112; Mark Read 207; Sipa Press/Rex Features 35; Tim Thompson/APA 198, 199, 201, 219, 227; Topham Picturepoint 30, 33; Tourism Hollywood 182; Tourism Niagara 67; Tourism Texas 152; Doug Traverso 178, 193; Gregory Wrona 107, 108, 111.

Cover picture: 4Corners Images

Contact us

At Berlitz we strive to keep our guides as accurate and up to date as possible, but if you find anything that has changed, or if you have any suggestions on ways to improve this guide, then we would be delighted to hear from you.

Berlitz Publishing, PO Box 7910, London SE1 1WE, England.
fax: (44) 20 7403 0290
email: berlitz@apaguide.co.uk
www.berlitzpublishing.com